On Earth and In Hell

Auf der Erde und in der Hölle

THOMAS BERNHARD

Translated from the German by
PETER WAUGH

A Bilingual Edition

THREE ROOMS PRESS

NEW YORK CITY

*Special thanks to the family of Thomas Bernhard, particularly
Dr. Peter and Anny Fabjan, and to Dr. Petra Hardt of Suhrkamp.
Deepest gratitude to Barbara Hutt for her gracious assistance
in making this project a reality. Also, sincere appreciation to
Peter Waugh for his indefatigable efforts and brilliant translations.
And deepest gratitude to Léone Jaffin for her kind help and ongoing
encouragement.*

On Earth and In Hell
(Auf der Erde und in der Hölle)
by Thomas Bernhard

Translated from the German
by Peter Waugh

ISBN: 978-1-941110-23-2 (trade paper)
ISBN: 978-1-941110-24-9 (ebook)
Library of Congress Control Number: 2015935227

COVER PHOTO:
Thomas Bernhard, Obernathal 1966
Photo: Johann Barth (© Copyright Sepp Dreissinger)

COVER AND BOOK DESIGN:
KG Design International
www.katgeorges.com

PUBLISHED BY:
Three Rooms Press, New York, NY
www.threeroomspress.com

DISTRIBUTED BY:
PGW/Perseus
www.pgw.com

Contents

Introduction

by Jaimy Gordon

AUTHOR, *LORD OF MISRULE*, NATIONAL BOOK AWARD WINNER

IF, AS IS OFTEN SAID, THE AUSTRIANS managed to duck official responsibility for their Nazi past, they loathed themselves in art no less for this. In the second half of the twentieth century, at shows of self-disgust for their own delight and edification, they were no slouches, and as long as the invective was home grown, by one of their own, it was as scandalously welcome as the ritual obscenities slung by professional insulters at initiates on the road from Athens to Eleusis.

There was an open niche in postwar Austrian letters for a vitriolic jester, and into this lacuna stepped Thomas Bernhard, twenty-five years old in the mid-fifties, with his damaged lungs, beggarly prospects, and bastard orphan's feelings of abandonment, his only family legacy being an obsession with the artist's glorious mission, handed down by his maternal grandfather, Johannes Freumbichler—whose name, by the way, sounds as ridiculous in German as it does in English. Freumbichler had been a mostly unsuccessful author of *Heimatromane*, popular novels about country villages, virtuous maids in braids and dirndls, "the poetry of pigs," of those jugs of homemade freshly fermented spirits, called *Most*, found in every farmer's cellar, of cows and wayside crosses, of village churches, weddings, and graveyards. The reader of *On Earth and In Hell* will not fail to notice the same imagery of the countryside in poem after poem by young Bernhard, although insistently laced with disgust and death and lamentation, and colored black where possible.

One of the great fiction writers of the twentieth century, Bernhard often reminds me, especially in his early books, of some mad, prophetic ranter at a fancy dinner who is surprised to find himself the life of the party. At the next party—or in the next book—the monologue is no less corrosive, but, by degrees, more brilliantly ironic and contrapuntal—and funnier. We become confident, in time, that Bernhard is managing his own mad show, for our shock but also for our entertainment. Was his grotesque jeremiad meant in jest all along? We don't quite know, and the uneasiness of not knowing makes us more, not less, warily fascinated.

It's true, you won't find many laughs in these poems, written in Bernhard's mid-twenties; and yet all the matter of the subsequent malicious laughter is there—the self-splitting disgust and nostalgia, the hyperbolic despair, the failed (desired but also scorned) glory, the juxtaposition of village idyll and doom, of scathing superiority and terminal stupidity, of sex, and nauseated frailty and exhaustion. Later on, in novel after novel, Bernhard speaks to, or through, the persona of some obsessive, flamboyantly vituperative, unrelentingly disgusted genius—a philosopher, or musician, or mathematician— who will become the ruin of all who are attached to him, as well as of himself. For me, the poems of *On Earth and In Hell* seem to be written not so much by Thomas Bernhard, as by the mad, theatrically cursing and suffering protagonist of a first novel that Thomas Bernhard never quite wrote, when Bernhard hadn't yet realized, perhaps, that his obsessions, dancing or shuffling along sadly in boiled-wool loden Alpine jackets to slightly out of tune brass-band music at all those pork-rich Flachgau weddings and funerals, were funny, horribly funny.

As soon as histrionic paradoxes like these were funneled into the voices of characters in his novels, readers began to protest, but also to laugh—in Austria to laugh with a furious sense of recognition. In more Pietistic Germany, the examination of identity requires a look inward, in the supposed direction of the conscience, a deep-seated organ distributed one to a person like the gall bladder. In Austria, as befits a Catholic former empire with its twin sacred masquerades of

Fasching (Carnival) and Burgtheater, contrition quite naturally expresses itself as a play of masks and mirrors, *personae*, alter egos. Even with an infinitely interchangeable mask of universal disgust, as in Bernhard, the style is finally a revel, the refrain: Yes, I am the guilty one, weak, selfish, base, even murderous, but what did you expect? Who isn't? Not only in Austria, it's always a fair question.

© Jaimy Gordon
Kalamazoo, Michigan
September 2015

Jaimy Gordon won the National Book Award in 2010 for her novel Lord of Misrule. *She is the American translator of German fiction writer and memoirist Maria Beig.*

Prologue

by Barbara Hutt

STAGE DIRECTOR AND CO-AUTHOR OF *THOMAS BERNHARD*

I HAVE WORKED ON THOMAS BERNHARD for so many years that he has become a part of my life. This is the reason why I wanted his poems to be known by the English speaking readers and I got permission from the half-brother of Thomas Bernhard and his wife to have them published by my American publisher friends, Peter Carlaftes and Kat Georges.

On the train taking me back to Paris, some fifteen years ago, I couldn't believe my eyes. Stunned by a book: the complete poems of Thomas Bernhard, which I had just bought in Germany. I had assumed I knew this author through and through. But here was a hypersensitive stranger, leading me through a heartwrenching journey, circles of hell punctuated with spring beams and unexpected bubbles of tenderness. A soul exposed to the very core, explosive.

Gone was the self-contained ironic author of novels and plays that my partner, Pierre Chabert[1], and I had been staging for years and whom we were now publishing a biography on[2]. As the German speaker in our couple, I could access Thomas Bernhard's poetry, never translated into French. I insisted on doing so despite the

---

1 French stage director, deceased in 2010, internationally renowned for his work on Thomas Bernhard and Samuel Beckett.

2 *Thomas Bernhard*, Pierre Cabert and Barbara Hutt (Minerve, 2002), a major book on his life and works, including testimonies of his closest friends and relatives.

dismissive comments the poems had thus far attracted in Berhard's native Austria: too rural, too youthful . . .

Diving ever deeper into the pages, I realized all this contempt was probably another expression of the dogged resentment the Austrians felt towards an author who, while attracting international praise, had relentlessly reminded them of a nauseating past: no, they had not been victims of Hitler, they had cheered him when he invaded their country and incorporated it into his Third Reich. So much dirt was poured over Thomas Bernhard, sometimes even literally: real manure was dumped on the entrance of a theater where, once again, he was questioning the unquestionable.

"Youthful" and "rural" his poetry certainly is. But not in the way his critics meant it, as this present edition hopefully reveals. It is the full version of *On Earth and In Hell*, Thomas Bernhardt's very first publication, in 1957, as a poet and, more importantly, as a writer. Thus far, he had only published the odd poem and dabbled in journalism, driving his editors nuts because, when covering trials, he would change the verdicts that didn't suit him.

But all the while, the fainthearted journalist had been writing the pages that follow, searching his soul, re-experiencing pangs of hunger in war-torn Austria, and questioning all, including his own capacity to write anything. A fierce inner battle where, while trying to uproot himself from his beloved native countryside, the illegitimate fatherless child writhes as an incarnation of sin and doubts the reality of his own voice.

Beloved countryside . . . a mixed feeling, though: at one with the elements, feet happily planted on pure soil, young Thomas despairs at the void and pettiness that lurk around him. He curses priests and confides in his unknown father, gone before he was even born. When the little boy asks who he is, the only answer he gets is a slap in the face. It is a dark world and a cold one, in a very real sense. During the freezing winters, Thomas watches an old man drape himself in a horse's skin before settling to perform a strange task: hitting the keys of a typewriter. His grandfather, a poet, worshipped by the child.

Will words save Thomas? Open up an escape? The night "stabs his heart." Inner cities beckon and burn. Words seem helpless. The young man gropes, flies them around, and hurls them at each other. Fireworks. Does fire work? Can you rise from your own cinders as an eighteen-year-old on a sanatorium bed, dying of tuberculosis, according to the doctors, when you learn that your beloved grandfather has just passed away? He will bequeath Thomas a bag and a suitcase. And the typewriter.

The young man's health would never be fully recovered. Often so ill he would disappear for long periods, shunning the outer world, earning himself a reputation for misanthropy. A misunderstanding, one of many.

© BARBARA HUTT
Paris, France
May 2015

My deepest thanks to Peter Fabjan, Thomas Bernhard's half-brother, and his wife, Anny Fabjan, to my recently deceased mother, Suzanne Wolff-Hutt, for translating the poems of Thomas Bernhard into French, and to Leone Jaffin and Youcef Douhi for their friendly and professional help.

Translator's Essay: *Bursting Upon the Scene*

by Peter Waugh

TRANSLATOR, *ON EARTH AND IN HELL*

THE BOOK YOU ARE HOLDING IN your hands is the first English translation of Thomas Bernhard's first volume of poetry: *On Earth and in Hell*. When it initially came out in German in 1957, entitled *Auf der Erde und in der Hölle* (originally published by Otto Müller Verlag in Salzburg), it was not only the twenty-six-year-old Austrian author's first book of poetry, but also the very first complete literary work of any kind that he had published[1].

With this first book of verse, Thomas Bernhard was knowingly following the well-trodden tradition of the German-language writer whose appearance on the literary scene had often been heralded by the publication of a volume of poems[2]. Later, after one or two other volumes and, ideally, having achieved a certain modicum of success, aspiring authors would move on to writing novels or plays (poetry being mistakenly regarded by critics and authors alike as the minor genre).[3]

It might be said that, like many great artists, Bernhard went on to simply mine ever deeper the gold seam of the themes of his greatest

---

1 Thomas Bernhard was born on February 9, 1931.

2 The same situation may of course also be observed in other literary cultures as well. One famous example from Irish literature: James Joyce's book of poems *Chamber Music* (1907).

3 *Frost* (novel, Suhrkamp, Frankfurt am Main, 1963); *Auslöschung* (novel, Suhrkamp, Frankfurt am Main, 1986); *Heldenplatz* (play, Suhrkamp, Frankfurt am Main, 1963).

"waltz" (*viz.* endlessly repeating the pattern of the masterly inner monologue in his novels, or making the puppets dance to the same socio-critical music of his plays—and some inklings of these qualities may even be gleaned here as he bursts onto the literary with this initial book of poems). Yet the author of *Frost,* of *Auslöschung,* and of *Heldenplatz* was without a doubt the most influential novelist and dramatist of post-war, late-twentieth-century Austrian literature.

Nonetheless, today, Thomas Bernhard is not primarily regarded as a poet, in the sense that some other great modern Austrian writers were (or are), of whom we might mention Christine Lavant, Ingeborg Bachmann, Erich Fried, Konrad Bayer, H. C. Artmann, Elfriede Mayröcker, Ernst Jandl, Gerhard Rühm, among many others—and Austrian literature does indeed proudly evince a wonderful array of modern poets of huge talent. Of course, some of the above also wrote novels and plays, but remained primarily poets. With Bernhard it was the other way round, as it was with Peter Handke, Wolfgang Bauer, Elfriede Jelinek, or Peter Turrini, all of whom became renowned novelists and/or playwrights, yet started off with highly esteemed volumes of verse when young, and ended up inhabiting other regions on the literary genre map. While this does not detract from the achievements of the poetry that they wrote, it does illustrate an ancient truth about the wild and youthful nature of poetry. More of which later.

In the case of Bernhard, he remained a poet in his later years only in spirit, since he did not publish any new poems after 1963 (i.e. some nine years after the publication of *Auf der Erde und in der Hölle*). This was the year when he began to establish himself as a novelist with the publication of *Frost*[4]. However, he did continue to rework and publish poems that had been written earlier, and in 1981 Suhrkamp brought out the volume *Ave Vergil,* containing poems written in 1959–60[5].

---

4 The act of turning his back on poetry may actually have been connected to the fact that, following the success of *Auf der Erde und in der Hölle* (1957) and the subsequent volumes *In Hora Mortis* (Otto Müller, Salzburg, 1958) and *Unter dem Eisen des Mondes* (Kiepenheuer & Witsch, Cologne, 1958) his fourth book of poems, which was to be entitled *Frost,* was for some reason, disappointingly rejected after long deliberations on the part of his earlier publishers, Otto Müller, in Salzburg. It seems that most of the 140 poems from this work remained unpublished. Although, during this period, Bernard did bring out one more book of poetry, entitled *Die Irren, Die Häftlinge* (privately printed in Klagenfurt in 1962), he decided to concentrate on composing his first novel. When it was eventually published, to huge acclaim, in Germany (Insel Verlag, Munich, 1963), it bore the same title that had been intended for the volume of verse: *Frost.*

5 See *Thomas Bernhard Gesammelte Gedichte,* ed. Volker Bohn (Suhrkamp Verlag, Frankfurt am Main, 1991), editorial note by Volker Bohn, p. 335–338.

This first book of poetry was greeted with an equal measure of acclaim and reserve on the part of critics, colleagues, and readers. The German writer and playwright Carl Zuckmayer wrote in a review of the book: "Perhaps these poems are the greatest discovery that I have made in our literature over the last ten years." Peter Hamm, encountering it as a young writer at the age of twenty, was totally enthralled by it, reviewing it in the Communistic journal *Geist und Tat* thus:

> "Not since Trakl—with the exception of Christine Lavant—has Austria seen the emergence of such an original poet as Thomas Bernhard. Every new sentence by him has the power to literally bowl one over, in such an elementary and consistently new manner does he confront the reader. Here poetry has once again ravished the poet, à la Rimbaud, has compelled him, obsessed by life though he be, to renounce life for the sake of poetry."[6]

Prior to the publication of *Auf der Erde und in der Hölle*, Bernhard had worked as a court reporter for a local newspaper, and had already published a few short stories and some of his poems in literary magazines, newspapers and anthologies. He had just begun to make some inroads into the literary scene in Vienna, and had evidently already attracted some attention, since the Austrian poet Ingeborg Bachmann, who was already an established member of the influential Gruppe 47 in Germany, remarked in response to Hamm's effusive commendation of *Auf der Erde und in der Hölle*, rather more coolly, that: "He—Bernhard—has already arrived, fully immersed in the urge to write his poems, but not yet in the poems themselves."[7]

Thomas Bernhard had already imbued the spirit of Rimbaud[8], Baudelaire and the French Symbolists, having read them while recuperating in various sanatoria from the tuberculosis which had developed from a severe pleurisy that he had caught working in a grocer's

---

6 Peter Hamm, review originally printed in *Geist und Tat*, 1957, here quoted from Peter Hamm's preface to Sind *Sie Gern Böse*, Thomas Bernhard/Peter Hamm (Suhrkamp Verlag, Berlin, 2011), p. 7. *Sind Sie Gern Böse* (*Do You Enjoy Being Malevolent?*) is an interview which Hamm conducted with Bernhard in 1976/77, but which the latter subsequently forbade him to publish, although it eventually came out in 2011.

7 Ingeborg Bachmann, *Ibid.* p. 7.

8 See the essay 'Jean Arthur Rimbaud. Zum 100. Geburtstag', in: *Die Wahrheit auf der Spur* (Suhrkamp Verlag, Berlin, 2011), originally a lecture given by Thomas Bernhard on November 9, 1954, at the Hotel Pitter in Salzburg, on the occasion of the 100th anniversary of Rimbaud's birth.

office (1947–1949) and which would plague him all his life and be the cause of his death. Furthermore, in the course of his theatre studies in Salzburg (1955–1957), he had become fascinated by the work of Antonin Artaud. Yet most evident here is the influence exerted by Georg Trakl (d. 1914), the most important Austrian poet of the early 20th century, especially for Austrian poets immediately after the Second World War. "Everyone was trying to write like Trakl at that time."[9]

So *Auf der Erde und in der Hölle* is Bernhard's entrance on the literary stage: and here he is, by turns intoxicated and agonized, ecstatic and melancholic, high on glory and deep in despair, scornful and imploring, misanthropic and compassionate—moods that would become familiar in other guises in his later work in other genres. These poems may be described as Tracklian, Rimbaudian and Artaudian in their moods and movement, but above all else they are Bernhardian—in fact, they are the first ever manifestation of such a quality and adjective. In them we see the very first bristling glimmer of an initiatory fire that would later be observed as the inexorably soaring ascent of a raging new star in the literary heavens.

AT THE START OF *EIN KIND* (*A Child*), the first part of Thomas Bernhard's autobiographical trilogy[10], there is a wonderfully amusing description of how, as an eight-year-old, he discovers a bicycle, mounts it, even though it is somewhat too big for him, and departs, daring to learn how to ride, and to his amazement finding it easy, so that he happily continues, intent on riding as far as his growing legs can carry him, maybe to visit his favorite aunt in Salzburg?—wherever that might be . . . until the chain breaks and he has to be rescued and brought back to his mother and face dire punishment. Whether the episode is actually true or not (one never really knows with Bernhard), this first volume of verse bears a certain similarity to the first part of that bicycle ride: here we see him daring, learning to ride, learning to write, and since he can ride/write very well, he immediately channels the Poetic Genius (in a Blakean sense), access to which had been gradually made available to him through years of constant educational contact with his beloved grandfather, the relatively unknown poet and author Johannes

---

9 Translation of a verbatim quote by the Austrian experimental prose poet Bodo Hell.
10 *Ein Kind* (Residenz Verlag, Salzburg, 1982).

Freumbichler (born in 1881), who by chance happened to die in the very same hospital in which Bernhard had come to recover from tuberculosis in February 1949. Yet his grandfather's lack of success was something the young poet's already feisty ambition was determined not to replicate.

Auf der Erde und in der Hölle is an attempt by a young poet—precociously talented and well aware of his skill—to capture the truth of his own experience in all its uniqueness and strangeness, employing meticulously crafted language in a wild and devil-may-care exploration of a path through his twisted emotional life and painful physical existence in order to gain some kind clarity of perception and find a balanced sense of wonder, beyond the forest and beyond the town. Even beyond the country village which was never really home. Already having experienced the humiliation of a difficult childhood involving a father who had fled his birth, a mother who was forced to be absent, even abroad, for long periods while working, years of upbringing by his beloved grandparents, but also years of maltreatment in a Nazi-run children's home in Germany, traumas of moving, separation, authoritarian education, fear of school, the war, bombings, bed-wetting, health problems . . . Now it is the late 1950s and here he is, an angry and desperate young man, pursuing the sublimation of sexual life into literature, the cannibalization of his own experience for the purposes of writing, trying out his repertoire of themes for size. Seeing how far he can go with his attacks on the various groups, institutions, areas of human activity, mentalities and attitudes that he sees as contributors to his own suffering in particular and that of society and the human race in general, yet without any incriminating mention of names. Later, in the novels and plays, the names too would be added, real names, just as the letters summoning him to court for libel would subsequently begin to arrive at his door.

Thomas Bernhard's poetry stands up to be counted, stands out with the uniqueness of his lamenting yet celebratory voice, unleashing his ire with relentless criticism of the fate of human beings, individuals lost in the mass madness of a senseless, vegetative and inane society. It is redolent of the sadness and joy of life's transience, the mind-wrenching predicament of being born into a world of enchanting beauty and cold calculating nature, mingled always with the presence of physical and emotional pain and the inevitability of death. Knowledge of this situation becomes lost to the sight of human beings, immolated, blindfolded by others and condemned to trudge the grooved track of sightless habit and ignorance.

The mood here is that of wise old youth celebrating its vision while railing against imminent loss, searching for transcendence and yearning for redemption, yet sensing that the verve of life is fast disappearing as the dead world of corrupt, helpless and insincere older generations bears down upon it with ever increasing speed and rapacity. Capture your perceptions quickly, for tomorrow they will be gone, forgotten as you drink society's contaminated water ever deeper, till eventually you see nothing. The young still know that there must be more to life than the mess they observe all around them, and poetry is one of the fastest, most direct natural ways to perceive a truth: here, that of ignorance in the midst of wonder at a mystery the world no longer nurtures, just as nature or society care nothing for human beings except as creatures of procreation or social units. On earth and in hell. What's the difference? None. Welcome to the beauties of life on earth and (on the flip side of the coin), the terrors of life in hell. Toss it again and see what goes up and what comes down this time around.

Thomas Bernhard was a relentless *agent provocateur*, a literary saboteur of the absurdly entrenched positions of a blinkered, mindcuffed post-war society; courter of controversy, delighter in the creation of ballooning scandals. With a wicked, knowing smirk on his lips as he looked the other way, he kept his distance, yet still came too close for comfort for half-repressed, barely post-Nazi Austria. Gleeful taunter of the knee-jerking gutter press and the far right (and even the conservatives), both of whom collaborated to stage demonstrations against the performance of his plays, calling for boycotts even though they were incapable of appreciating his humor and had hardly read or seen the plays.

Bernhard, too, was a man of apparent contradictions: championed by the left, abhorred by the right, he remained highly critical of all the hypocrisy that came within reach of the withering fire of his perceptive wit. Yet after he died[11], it became known that he himself had been a lifelong member of the rather conservative Austrian Farmers' Association. In accordance with his last will and testament, his funeral

---

11 On February 12, 1989. Coincidentally, the evening of February 11 had been the anniversary of the death of his grandfather, who had passed away exactly 40 years beforehand.

was held not only in private but also in secret, with no public announcement of his death being made until after he had already been buried. It was also declared that none of his works should be performed or published in Austria until one hundred years after his death. An expertly planned masterstroke of revenge, a guffaw from beyond the grave. A big swipe at those whom he regarded as his tormentors, namely "the great killjoys of life" in the guise of the political establishment[12]. However, the ban was revoked within almost ten years of his death, when the Thomas Bernhard Foundation was formed in 1998—as he may all-too-well have known it would be . . .

I would like to offer my thanks to the Austrian Federal Chancery, namely the Section for Literature, and in particular Dr. Robert Stocker and Gerhard Auinger, for their support in financing the execution of this translation. Of course also to the publishers, Peter Carlaftes and Kat Georges, for all their work in making the publication possible and for their endless patience and help in steering it through to the end. Also to the Thomas Bernhard Estate and the Thomas Bernhard Archive for granting the translation rights. Further, to my wife, the poetess Hanane Aad for her support and encouragement, and also to the Austrian authors Gabriele Petricek, Bodo Hell and Christian Katt for their occasional assistance in clarifying the ambivalent nature and poetic ambiguities of a few semantic strands.

I can only hope that these translations would have met with Thomas Bernhard's approval. I have certainly enjoyed the journey of translating the original poems. I hope you will equally enjoy the journey of reading the results, in all their wild vibrancy of life.

© PETER WAUGH
Vienna, Austria
April 2015

---

12 See *Thomas Bernhard* by Hans Höller (Rowohlt, Reinbeck bei Hamburg, 1993), pp. 7–17 and p. 131.

On Earth
and In Hell

Auf der Erde und in der Hölle

On Earth and in Hell

Der Tag der Gesichter

Morgen ist der Tag der Gesichter. Sie werden
   sich erheben wie Staub
   und in Gelächter ausbrechen.
Morgen ist der Tag der Gesichter, die in
   die Kartoffelerde gefallen sind. Ich kann
   nicht leugnen, daß ich
   an diesem Sterben der Triebe schuldig bin.
Ich bin schuldig!
Morgen ist der Tag der Gesichter, die meine Qual
   auf der Stirn tragen,
   die mein Tagwerk besitzen.
Morgen ist der Tag der Gesichter, die wie Fleisch
   auf der Kirchhofsmauer tanzen
   und mir die Hölle zeigen.
   Warum muß ich die Hölle sehen? Gibt es keinen
                             anderen Weg
  zu Gott?

Eine Stimme: Es gibt keinen anderen Weg! Und dieser
                                     Weg
  führt über den Tag der Gesichter,
  er führt durch die Hölle.

The Day of the Faces

Tomorrow is the day of the faces. They shall
   arise like dust
   and break out in laughter.
Tomorrow is the day of the faces that fell
   into the potato earth. I cannot
   deny that I
   am guilty of the death of these shoots.
I am guilty!
Tomorrow is the day of the faces that bear
   my torment on their brows
   and own my day's work.
Tomorrow is the day of the faces that dance
   like flesh on the churchyard wall
   and show me Hell.
   Why do I have to see Hell? Is there no
                       other way

   to God?

A Voice: There is no other way! And this
                      way

   leads via the day of the faces,
   it leads through Hell.

HINTER DEN BÄUMEN IST EINE
ANDERE WELT

※

BEHIND THE TREES IS
ANOTHER WORLD

Mein Urgrossvater
war Schmalzhändler

Mein Urgroßvater war Schmalzhändler,
und heute
kennt ihn noch jeder
zwischen Henndorf und Thalgau,
Seekirchen und Köstendorf,
und sie hören seine Stimme
und rücken
zusammen an seinem Tisch,
der auch der Tisch des Herrn war.
1881, im Frühjahr,
entschied er sich für das Leben: er pflanzte
Wein an der Hauswand
und rief die Bettler zusammen;
seine Frau, Maria, die mit dem schwarzen Band,
schenkte ihm weitere tausend Jahre.
Er erfand die Musik der Schweine
und das Feuer der Bitternis,
er sprach vom Wind
und von der Hochzeit der Toten.
Er würde mir kein Stück Speck geben
für meine Verzweiflungen.

My Great-Grandfather
Was a Lardseller

My great-grandfather was a lardseller,
and even today
he's known to all who live
between Henndorf and Thalgau,
Seekirchen and Köstendorf,
and they hear his voice
and edge
closer together at his table,
which was also the table of the Lord.
In 1881, in spring,
he decided in favor of life: he planted
vines by the house wall
and gathered together the beggars;
his wife, Maria, she of the black ribbon,
granted him another thousand years.
He invented the music of pigs
and the fire of bitterness,
he spoke of the wind
and of the wedding of the dead.
He wouldn't give me a scrap of bacon
for all my despair.

Auf den schwarzen Truhen
der Bauernerde

Auf den schwarzen Truhen der Bauernerde
    steht geschrieben, daß ich sterben muß im Winter,
verlassen von meinen Sonnen und vom Geraune der Kübel,
    der vollgemolkenen,
Qual und Ende sprechend unter den Schlägen des Märzwinds,
    der mich vernichtet mit dem Gedanken
an die Apfelblüten und den Zauber der Tennen!
    Niemals habe ich eine Nacht zerstört mit Schimpfworten
und Tränen, aber diese Zeit, diese unsinnige Zeit,
    wird mich auslöschen
mit ihrer trockenen, messerscharfen Poesie!
    Ich werde nicht nur Verlassenheit erdulden müssen, sondern
das Vieh meiner Väter und Mütter durch die Jahrtausende treiben!
    Ich werde Regen erschaffen müssen
und Schnee und Mütterlichkeit
    für meine Verbrechen und den Zorn rühmen,
der mir das Getreide auf den eigenen Feldern ruiniert!
    Ich werde die Händler und Samstaghuren in einem
                       Waldstück zusammenrufen,
und dieses Land, dieses traurige Land,
    ihrer wilden Verzweiflung schenken!
Ich werde tausend Sonnen hereinkommen lassen in meinen
    Hunger! Morgen werde ich
Vergängliche erschaffen für die Unsterblichkeit,
    nahe der Brunnen und Türme und fern
der Handwerker,
    in einer Frühe, die meiner Leiden überdrüssig ist
und in der nichts geschieht als der Heimgang der Sterne . . .
    . . . dort will ich mit den Verzweifelten sprechen
und alles zurücklassen,
    was Verachtung, Bitternis und Trauer war auf dieser Erde.

On the Black Chests
of Country Earth

On the black chests of country earth
    it is written that I shall die in winter,
abandoned by my suns and by the murmur of buckets,
    full after milking,
speaking of torment and death beneath the blows of the March wind,
    which destroys me with the thought
of apple blossoms and the magic of threshing floors!
    I have never destroyed a night with swearing
and tears, yet this time, this nonsensical time,
    will eradicate me
with its dry poetry, keen as a knife!
    Not only shall I have to suffer abandonment, but
drive my father's and mother's cattle through the millennia!
    I shall have to create rain
and snow and motherhood
    for my crimes, and praise the wrath
that ruins the crops on my own fields!
    I shall gather together the sellers and Saturday whores on a patch
                             of forest,
and grant them this land, this sad land,
    of their wild despair!
I shall let one thousand suns enter my hunger!
    Tomorrow I shall
create transience for immortality,
    near the wells and towers and far
from the craftsmen,
    in an early morning weary of my suffering
and in which nothing happens but the passing-away of the stars . . .
    . . . there I shall speak to the despairing
and leave behind everything
that was full of scorn, bitterness and sorrow on this earth.

Novemberopfer

Ich bin unwürdig dieser Felder und Furchen,
    unwürdig dieses Himmels, der seine wilden Zeichen
in mein Gedächtnis für ein neues Jahrtausend schreibt,
    unwürdig dieser Wälder, deren Schauer
mit den Gewittern der Städte hereinbricht in mein Altern.
    Ich bin unwürdig dieser Mütter am Abhang und unwürdig
der Bauern, die ihren Tag durchwühlen
    mit Kühen und Birnbäumen, Suff und Sensen.
Ich bin unwürdig dieser Berge und Kirchtürme,
    unwürdig einer einzigen Sternnacht
und unwürdig eines jeden Bettlers Fußpfad,
    der in Traurigkeit endet.
Ich bin unwürdig dieses Grases, das meine Glieder kühlt,
    der Baumstämme, die der Norden
in ihr grausames Gebrechen treibt mit dem Regen
    und den Schatten der Burschen,
die dem Most ihr Novemberopfer darbringen
    unter den schwarzen Hügeln, die meine Vergänglichkeit tragen.
Ich bin unwürdig dieser Prozessionen,
    die der Mai hervorbringt zwischen blühenden Apfelbäumen,
der Milch und des Honigs, des Ruhms und der Fäulnis,
    die mir zugesichert sind.
Ich bin unwürdig unter Pfarrern, Metzgern und Händlern,
    unwürdig den Weissagungen dieser Gärten,
unwürdig des Sonntags, der seinen süßen Qualm ins Blau spuckt.
    Unwürdig bin ich verlassener rotgesprenkelter Mädchen
in dieser jahrtausendealten Landschaft,
    deren Brot schmeckt nach Hunger und Toten,
Eitelkeit und dem Kummer der Mütter,
    die ihrer Qual nicht entfliehen können,
der Qual der Vergessenen, die die Sonne auf den Feldern verbrennt.

November Sacrifice

I am unworthy of these fields and furrows,
   unworthy of this sky that writes its wild signs
in my memory for a new millennium,
   unworthy of these woods, whose shiver
breaks into my maturing mind with the storms of towns.
   I am unworthy of these mothers on the hillside and unworthy
of the farmers who rummage through their day
   with cows and pear trees, booze and scythes.
I am unworthy of these mountains and church spires,
   unworthy of a single starry night
and unworthy of any beggar's footpath
   that ends in sadness.
I am unworthy of this grass that cools my limbs,
   of the tree trunks whose hideous affliction
the north deepens with its rain
   and the shadows of boys
who offer up November sacrifices to the young wine
   beneath the black hills that bear my transience.
I am unworthy of these processions
   that May brings forth between blossoming apple trees,
of the milk and the honey, of the glory and the decay,
   of which I am assured.
I am unworthy among priests, butchers and sellers,
   unworthy of the wise words of these gardens,
unworthy of Sunday, which spits its sweet fumes into the blue.
   Unworthy am I of abandoned red-speckled girls
in this landscape thousands of years old,
   whose bread tastes of hunger and the dead,
vanity and the grief of the mothers
   who could not escape their torment,
the torment of the forgotten, who are scorched by the sun in the fields.

Unwürdig bin ich der Amsel, unwürdig dem Knarren
des Mühlrads,
unwürdig treib ich mein Spiel an den Ufern des Flusses,
der von den Dörfern nichts wissen will.
Ich bin unwürdig dieser Seelen, die in Wolken und Büschen
zueinander sprechen von der blühenden Erde,
von des sterbenden Himmels Musik,
von den großen Verlassenheiten, über die Hügel huschend,
ungeduldig vorauseilend stürmischen Wintern der Welt.

Unworthy am I of the blackbird, unworthy of the creaking of
                                       the millwheel,
unworthy I play my game on the banks of the river,
    which refuses to have anything to do with the villages.
I am unworthy of these souls in the clouds and the bushes
    that speak to one another of the flourishing earth,
of the music of the dying heavens,
    of the great abandonments, scurrying over the hills,
anxiously hurrying ahead of the world's stormy winters.

Fäulnis

Unvergänglich wie die Sonne sah ich die Erde,
    als ich zurück in den Schlaf ging, den Vater zu suchen,
der des letzten Windes Botschaft brachte
    in meine Erbärmlichkeit, die seinen Ruhm betrübte,
den Ruhm, von dem er sagte: »Die großen Geschicke
    scheitern für morgen . . .«
Unvergänglich standen die Wälder, die einst die Nacht
    erfüllten mit ihren Klagen und ihrer Rede
von Most und Untergang. Nur der Wind
    war über den Ähren, als lebte der Frühling
mitten in dieser süßen Fäulnis.
    Der Schnee verhielt sich feindlich und ließ
meine Glieder erschauern beim Anblick
    des unruhigen Nordens, der einem riesigen
                      unerschöpflichen
Friedhof glich, dem Friedhof der Gefangenen
    dieser Errungenschaft, die sich
in jedes Wegkreuz einschlich, in jeden Ackerstein
    und in alle Landstraßen und Kirchen, deren Türme sich
gegen Gott erhoben, und gegen die Hochzeitsgesellschaft,
    die um ihr Weinfaß hockte, um es
auszutrinken mit Schweinsgelächter.
    Wie sah ich diese Toten im Dorf auf den Brettern
mit angeschwollenen Bäuchen rotes Fleisch essen,
    die Hymnen des Märzenbiers lallen,
die Fäulnis, die durch den Gastgarten schlich
    unter dem trägen Gebrüll der Posaune . . .
Ich hörte den langsamen Atem der Verkommenheit
    zwischen den Hügeln . . .

Decay

Everlasting, like the sun, I saw the earth
    as I returned to sleep, in search of the father
who brought the last wind's message
    to my abject state, which grieved his glory,
the glory of which he said: "Great destinies
    fail for tomorrow . . ."
Everlasting stood the woods, which once filled
    the night with their laments and their talk
of young wine and doom. Only the wind
    was above the ears of corn, as if spring lived
in the midst of this sweet decay.
    The snow, acting like an adversary, made
my limbs shiver at the sight
    of the fretful north, resembling a huge
                            inexhaustible
graveyard, a graveyard of the prisoners
    of this achievement that crept
into every wayside cross, into every fieldstone
    and all country roads and churches, whose spires
rose up against God, and against the wedding society
    which sat around its wine barrel, intent
on drinking it dry to the sound of swinish laughter.
    How I saw all these village dead, bellies swollen,
eating red meat on the boards,
    slurring their hymns to the March beer,
and the decay which crept through the tavern garden
    beneath the sluggish bellow of the trumpet . . .
I heard the slow breath of debauchery
    between the hills . . .

Unvergänglich wie die Sonne sah ich die Erde,
deren August krank und unwiederbringlich war
    für mich und meine Brüder, die ihr Handwerk
besser gelernt haben als ich, der ich
    von Millionen Bettelschaften gequält bin und keinen
Baum für meine verrückten Gespräche mehr finde.
    Ich ging aus einer Nacht der Hölle
in eine Nacht des Himmels,
    nicht wissend, wer mein Leben zerschlagen muß,
bevor es zu spät ist, von Ruhm und Tapferkeit zu sprechen,
    von der Armut und den irdischen Verzweiflungen
des Fleisches, das mich vernichten wird . . .

Everlasting, like the sun, I saw the earth,
its August sick and irretrievable
    for me and my brothers—they learned
their trades better than I, tormented as I am
    by millions of beggarly things and now unable
to find even a tree for my crazy conversations.
    I left a night of hell
to enter a night of heaven,
    not knowing who would have to shatter my life
before it were too late to speak of glory and bravery,
    of the poverty and earthly despair
of the flesh that will destroy me . . .

In den Dörfern des Flachgaues

Nur Schatten stehen da, wo du die ersten Händler
gesehn hast, ihren Dreck hinter den Zähnen, die Schuhe,
die deinen Augen zu groß und unerklärlich waren,
nur Schatten stehen da, wo Kirchen sich öffneten und
                                        Greise ihren Ruhm
vergruben für ein besseres Leben,
als lebten sie nur für die Glieder und für Rauch und Wein
im Fleisch der süßen Bauernstuben.

Nur Schatten stehen da, wo sie den Honig verwässerten
und kranke Kühe an ruhmlos graue Städte abver-
                                        kauften, wo sie
den Müttern Gras und Leben raubten und
ihre Kinder sterben lehrten auf verlassenen Hügeln.
Nur Schatten stehen da und unwirtliche Bänke, die
                                        meinem Fleisch,
so sehr du dich auch plagst, den Ruhm nicht lassen,
der ihm gebührt nach seinen Fahrten.

Nur Schatten stehen da, wo sie die Falter nicht rühmen
und nicht die Poesie des Schweins und nicht den Tag
der Krüge und der Dämmerung, die aus den Wäldern
in ihre Schwermut eintritt, wo sie nicht rühmen
Meere, Städte, Krieger andrer Länder und nicht weinen
auf ungelöschtem Tag in den versperrten Tempeln, wo
                                        Sonne nur
auf kurz die staubigen Trümmer der Welt erreicht.

In the Villages of the Flachgau

Only shadows stand there, where you saw the first sellers,
the dirt behind their teeth, the shoes
too large and inexplicable for your eyes,
only shadows stand there, where churches opened

                                        and old men
buried their glory for a better life,
as if living only for their limbs, and for smoke and wine
in the flesh of sweet farmhouse parlors.

Only shadows stand there, where they watered down the honey
and sold off sick cows to inglorious gray towns,

                                        where they
robbed the mothers of grass and life and
on deserted hillsides taught their children to die.
Only shadows stand there and inhospitable benches,
which, however you may toil, still refuse my flesh the glory
that it so deserves after all its journeys.

Only shadows stand there, where they do not glorify
the butterflies, nor the poetry of pigs, nor the day
of jugs and of the twilight that enters their melancholy
from the woods, where they do not glorify
oceans, cities, or the warriors of other lands, and do not weep
by unextinguished day in the barred temples, where

                                        the sun but
fleetingly reaches the dusty rubble of the world.

Nur Schatten stehen da, wo sie die Träume trieben, des
                              Bluts nicht überdrüssig
und der Trauer, wo sie auf Märkte gingen, krank vor
                              Fleisch und vom Verspielen,
in Kirchen und zum Tanz, den Pfarrern oft zum Ekel, doch
ihrer Herkunft wohl zum Ruhm, und wo sie nächtlich
in ihren Betten horchten nach der Vergänglichkeit,
                                                 die sie
uns übertrugen in die Welt, die nicht mehr ihre ist.

Only shadows stand there, where they drove the dreams,
                                unweary of the blood
and the sorrow, where they went to markets, sick of the flesh
                                and of gaming,
into churches and to the dance, often to the nausea
                                of the priest, yet
to the likely glory of their ancestry, and where at night
they listened out in their beds for the transience that they
passed down to us, in this world that is no longer theirs.

Nieder geht der Regen
auf die schwarzen Wälder

Nieder geht der Regen auf die schwarzen Wälder,
Türen schließen sich zu meinen Stunden
so, als wäre ich nicht aus der Nacht gestiegen,
aus den Tiefen dieses grauen Tagwerks,
zornig, mit den letzten Freunden meiner
schwachen, niederträchtigen Seele,
die schon meines Vaters krankes Schicksal trug.

Nieder geht der Regen auf die schwarzen Wälder,
hör den Schrei, der deiner Sonne gilt, der müden,
die sich seltsam klagend durch die nassen Stämme
treiben läßt von einem bittern Abendwind.
Aus den hungrigen und trüben Augen steigen
nachts die Wunder dieser frühen Tage
und die Glieder strecken sich unter den Dächern
in den Fängen deiner trägen Poesie.

Nieder geht der Regen auf die schwarzen Wälder
und ich such den Traum, den ich noch gestern
lobte und der meine nassen Augen
niederdrückte auf das Bett im kalten Zimmer,
wo das Uhrwerk meine Welt zerstörte,
auch den letzten süßen Hauch des Friedens,
der meiner geliebten Bauernerde galt.

Down Comes the Rain
on the Black Woods

Down comes the rain on the black woods,
and doors close upon my hours,
quite as if I had not climbed from the night,
from the depths of this gray day's work,
angry, together with the last friends of my
feeble, malicious soul,
which already bore my father's sick fate.

Down comes the rain on the black woods,
hear the cry, made to your sun, the tired one,
which lets itself be driven, strangely plaintive,
through wet tree trunks by a bitter evening wind.
From hungry, troubled eyes there ascend
at night the marvels of these early days
and limbs stretch out beneath the roofs
in the clutches of your languid poetry.

Down comes the rain on the black woods
and I seek the dream that only yesterday
I praised and which pressed my wet eyes
down onto the bed in the cold room,
where clockwork destroyed my world,
and with it the last sweet breath of peace,
breathed for my beloved country earth.

Was werde ich tun . . .

Was werde ich tun,
    wenn keine Scheune mehr für mein Dasein bettelt,
wenn das Heu in nassen Dörfern verbrennt,
    ohne mein Leben zu krönen?
Was werde ich tun,
    wenn der Wald nur in meiner Phantasie wächst,
wenn die Bäche nur mehr leere, ausgewaschene Adern sind?

Was werde ich tun,
    wenn keine Botschaft mehr kommt aus den Gräsern?
Was werde ich tun,
    wenn ich vergessen bin von allen, von allen . . . ?

What Will I Do . . .

What will I do
    when no barn begs for my presence,
when the hay burns in wet villages
    without crowning my life?
What will I do
    when the forest grows only in my imagination,
when the streams are but empty, washed-out veins?

What will I do
    when no more messages come from the grasses?
What will I do
    when I've been forgotten by all, by all . . . ?

Bringt mir Schnaps, Ruhm und Liebe

Bringt mir Schnaps, denn ich will vergessen!
    Vertun will ich heute
alle Geschöpfe in mir und alle Qual,
    –dazu esse ich Fisch und ein Stück vom Schwein!

Bringt mir Ruhm, dann kann ich mich ruhig töten,
    bevor meine Seele aufschwillt
und mein stolzes Gehirn sich bläht
    und alle mich Narren begaffen!

Bringt mir eure Liebe an den Tisch,
    ich will sie trinken, schwimmend tief im Himmel,
hundert Krüge, tausend Krüge, alle Krüge der Welt, –
    ersaufen will ich in eurer Liebe.

Bring Me Hard Liquor, Glory and Love

Bring me hard liquor, for I wish to forget!
    Today, I wish to have done
with all my inner creatures and all torment—
    and I'll eat fish and a piece of pork!

Bring me glory, so I can kill myself in peace,
    before my soul becomes bloated
and my haughty brain distends,
    and they all gawk at me like idiots!

Bring to my table your love,
    I want to drink it, swimming deep in the sky,
hundred jugs, thousand jugs, all the jugs in the world—
    I want to drown in your love.

Gefangen

Der Rabe schreit.
    Er hat mich gefangen.
Immer muß ich in seinem Schrei
    durch das Land ziehn.
Der Rabe schreit.
    Er hat mich gefangen.
Gestern saß er im Acker und fror
    und mein Herz mit ihm.
Immer schwärzer wird mein Herz,
    denn es ist von schwarzen Flügeln
zugedeckt.

Caught

The crow cries.
    He has caught me.
In his cry I must forever
    travel the country.
The crow cries.
    He has caught me.
Yesterday he sat in the field and froze
    and my heart with him.
My heart grows ever blacker,
    covered over
by black wings.

Der Morgen trägt einen großen Sack

Der Morgen trägt einen großen Sack.
  Ich sage zu ihm: du bist so alt,
daß du mich nicht verachten brauchst.
  Deine Schuhe sind zerrissen.
Dein Rock hat einmal mir gehört –

  Ich sitze im Loch und erwarte dich,
nicht wie die Greisin, nicht wie die Kinder, nicht
  wie der Pfarrer, der nach der Predigt
zum Wein heruntersteigt und die Erde vertauscht.
  Ich empfange dich mit der Peitsche,
zitternd, gemein und zerbrechlich
  wie eine Distel im Sonnenrand.

Morning Carries a Big Sack

Morning carries a big sack.
    I say to him: you are so old,
you need not scorn me.
    Your shoes are in tatters.
Your coat was once mine.

    I sit in the hole and await you,
not like an old woman, nor like children, nor
    like the priest who, after his sermon,
descends to the wine, exchanging the earth.
    I receive you with my whip,
shaking, mean and fragile
    like a thistle at the edge of the sun.

Der Abend ist mein Bruder . . .

I
Der Abend ist mein Bruder, denn ich habe gesehn,
wie der Baum sich nach mir umdrehte,
denn ich habe gehört,
wie die Krüge der Bauern zerplatzten
und der Wein in ihre Gesichter spritzte,
die Jesus am Kreuz beschuldigten.

II
Ich werde fortgehen und ihre Füße waschen
und ihren Wein in neue Krüge füllen!
Ich werde mich auf den Marktplatz stellen und warten,
bis sie mir meinen Anzug herunterreißen
und meine Schuhe ins Fleisch schlagen,
mit denen ich hundert Jahre vorausgegangen bin.

Evening Is My Brother . . .

I
Evening is my brother, for I have seen
how the tree turns round after me,
and I have heard
how the jugs of the farmers broke
and the wine splattered their faces
when they blamed Jesus on the Cross.

II
I shall go out and wash their feet
and fill new jugs with their wine!
I shall stand in the market place and wait
till they tear down my suit
and beat into my flesh the shoes
in which I've walked a hundred years ahead.

Krähen

Bald kommt der Herbst und rettet die Vögel,
in finsteren Stuben sammeln Bruder und Schwester
die Körner für die Wintersmahlzeit.
Im schwarzen Dorf ist das Schwein angekettet.
Im Acker verenden die Krähen des Schmerzes.
Wir trinken das Bier der Verzweiflung
und falten die Hände vor der Verachtung des Vaters.
Die Erde schmeckt von den Schnüren des Fleisches.
Rauch steigt über die Höfe
und läßt die Furcht der besoffenen Bauern zurück.
Der Brunnenschenkel krächzt vor dem morschen Fenster . . .
Ich aber fürchte mich nicht.

Crows

Soon fall will come and save the birds,
in dark rooms brother and sister gather
grains for the winter meal.
In the black village the pig has been chained.
In the field crows perish in pain.
We drink the beer of despair
and fold our hands against the scorn of the father.
Earth tastes of the ropes of the flesh.
Smoke rises above the farmyards
and leaves behind it the drunken farmers' fear.
The well's axle croaks outside the rotten window . . .
Yet I am not afraid.

Hinter den Bäumen ist eine andere Welt

Hinter den Bäumen ist eine andere Welt,
der Fluß bringt mir die Klagen,
der Fluß bringt mir die Träume,
der Fluß schweigt, wenn ich am Abend in den Wäldern
vom Norden träume . . .

Hinter den Bäumen ist eine andere Welt,
die mein Vater vertauscht hat für zwei Vögel,
die meine Mutter heimtrug in einem Korb,
die mein Bruder im Schlaf verlor, als er sieben Jahr alt
was und müde . . .

Hinter den Bäumen ist eine andere Welt,
ein Gras, das nach Trauer schmeckt, eine schwarze Sonne,
ein Mond der Toten,
eine Nachtigall, die nicht aufhört zu klagen
von Brot und Wein
und Milch in großen Krügen
in der Nacht der Gefangenen.

Hinter den Bäumen ist eine andere Welt,
sie gehen in langen Furchen hinunter
in die Dörfer, in die Wälder der Jahrtausende,
morgen fragen sie nach mir,
nach der Musik meiner Gebrechen,
wenn der Weizen fault, wenn nichts von gestern
geblieben ist, von ihren Zimmern, Sakristeien und Wartesälen.

Ich will sie verlassen. Mit keinem
will ich mehr sprechen,
sie haben mich verraten, der Acker weiß es, die Sonne
wird mich verteidigen, ich weiß,
ich bin zu spät gekommen . . .

Behind the Trees Is Another World

Behind the trees is another world,
the river brings me laments,
the river brings me dreams,
the river grows silent when, in the evening forests,
I dream of the north . . .

Behind the trees is another world,
which my father exchanged for two birds,
which my mother carried home in a basket,
which my brother lost in his sleep, when seven years
                                        old and tired . . .

Behind the trees is another world,
a grass which tastes of sorrow, a black sun,
a moon of the dead,
a nightingale never ceasing to lament
about bread and wine
and milk in big jugs
in the night of the prisoners.

Behind the trees is another world,
they run down in long furrows
to the villages, to the forests of the millennia,
tomorrow they will ask about me,
about the music of my affliction,
when the wheat rots, when nothing of yesterday
has remained, of their rooms, sacristies or waiting halls.

I want to leave them. Don't want to speak
with any of them any more,
they have betrayed me, the field knows it, the sun
will defend me, I know,
I have come too late . . .

Hinter den Bäumen ist eine andere Welt,
dort ist ein anderer Kirtag,
im Kessel der Bauern schwimmen die Toten und um die Tümpel
schmilzt leise der Speck von den roten Skeletten,
dort träumt keine Seele mehr vom Mühlrad,
und der Wind versteht
nur den Wind . . .

Hinter den Bäumen ist eine andere Welt,
das Land der Fäulnis, das Land
der Händler,
eine Landschaft der Gräber laß hinter dir
und du wirst vernichten, grausam schlafen
und trinken und schlafen
vom Morgen zum Abend, vom Abend zum Morgen
und nichts mehr verstehn, nicht den Fluß und nicht die Trauer;
denn hinter den Bäumen
    morgen,
und hinter den Hügeln,
    morgen,
ist eine andere Welt.

Behind the trees is another world,
another country fair is going on there,
in the farmer's pot the dead swim, while round the ponds
the fat melts quietly from red skeletons,
no soul still dreams of the mill wheel there,
and the wind understands
only the wind . . .

Behind the trees is another world,
the country of decay, the country
of sellers—
leave a landscape of graves behind you
and you will destroy, sleep horribly
and drink and sleep
from morning to evening, from evening to morning
and no longer understand a thing, not the river and not the sorrow;
because behind the trees
    tomorrow,
and behind the hills,
    tomorrow,
is another world.

DIE AUSGEBRANNTEN STÄDTE

※

THE BURNT-OUT TOWNS

Die Städte hinter den Tümpeln

Wir haben die Städte hinter den Tümpeln
nie gesehn und nie die mürbe Trauer
der Verlassenheiten dieser kranken Menschen,
nie den Schmerz gespürt unter den Flügeln
schwarzer Vögel, die vorüberzogen
nach dem Spiel des qualvollen Oktober,
der sein Lied aus fernen Schloten schickt.

Wir haben die Städte hinter den Tümpeln
nie gesehn und nie das einsame Sterben
vieler Menschen, die noch neunzehnhundertvier
auf dem Tanzboden zu Hause waren
und in engen Zimmern einen Tag verblühen
und die Nacht aus finstern Gängen stürzen sahen
so, als wäre diese Erde traurig.

Wir haben die Städte hinter den Tümpeln
nie gesehn und nie das Klagen der Frauen
gehört, die in den Zimmern ihre Kleider
und ihre Bücher reinigten vom Staub der langen Jahre.
Nie hat einer von uns diesen Ruhm gesehn,
der auf weißen Mittagsplätzen stirbt unter den Klängen
einer hungrigen Konzertkapelle.

The Towns Beyond the Ponds

We've never seen the towns beyond the ponds
and never seen the brittle sorrow
of bereavement of these sick people,
never sensed the pain beneath the wings
of black birds that were passing by
after the game of torturous October,
which sends its song from distant chimneys.

We've never seen the towns beyond the ponds
and never seen the lonely deaths
of the many people who in nineteen-o-four
were still at home on the dance floor
and in pokey rooms saw a day bloom and fade
and night fall from dark corridors
as if this earth were sad.

We've never seen the towns beyond the ponds
and never heard the lament of the women
who in their rooms cleaned their clothes
and their books from the dust of long years.
None of us have ever seen this glory
which dies on white midday squares
beneath the sounds of a hungry concert band.

Bruchstücke
aus einer sterbenden Stadt

I
Wenn ich müde bin, roll ich mein Hirn auf den Platz
und lasse die Füße trampeln und die Gemeinheit der
                                    Metzger psalmieren.
Aus dem Loch eines Straßenbahnzuges schaue ich in den Himmel,
vom Zittern der Blätter verwirrt und vom Lippen-
                                    stülpen der Mädchen.
Ich flüchte in ein Milchgeschäft, wo sie traurig ihr
                                    Frühstück trinken
und an die Sonne denken, die nicht mehr kommt.
In grauen Mänteln schlafen sie und ahnen den Tod
vieler grüner Hügel.

II
Ich höre die Stimmen der Vögel unter dem Himmel
und das Geplätscher des Baches.
Ich schleppe unser verlassenes Dorf herein
und lasse die Milch aus Millionen Eutern jubeln!
Ich werfe tausend Münzen in die Hochzeitskapelle,
     die den besoffenen Bauern Ruhm bringt . . .

III
Die Lichter tönen wie rotes Fleisch in den Mitternachtsgassen,
und doch ist meine Sprache die Sprache des Winds,
der über den Anger bläst wie am ältesten Tag,
der die Greuel der Wüsten bringt und die Sehnsucht der
                                 trunkenen Palmbäume
nach dem Acker meines Vaters.

Fragments
from a Dying Town

I
When I am tired, I roll my brain onto the square
and let my feet stamp, and psalm the butchers' meanness.
From the hole of a tram I gaze up into the sky,
confused by the tremble of leaves and the girls'
                                        out-turned lips.
I flee into a milk shop, where they drink their
                                        breakfast sadly
and think of the sun that no longer comes.
They sleep in gray coats and foresee the death
of many green hills.

II
I hear the voices of birds beneath the sky
and the babble of the stream.
I drag our deserted village into it
and let the milk of a million udders rejoice!
I throw a thousand coins into the wedding chapel,
    which brings the drunken farmers glory . . .

III
The lights sound like red flesh in the midnight streets,
and yet my language is the language of the wind
which blows over the meadow as on the oldest day,
which brings the horrors of the desert and the desire
                                        of drunken palm trees
to my father's field.

IV

Ich esse mein Brot auf einem Fensterplatz und
schaue in ihr Gesicht, das dem Fleisch der Löwen gleicht
und der Vernichtung.
Ich sehe ihr Hirn abtropfen auf den verkommenen
                    Teppich der Bauerndörfer,
die soviel Schmerz nie getrunken haben wie in diesen Tagen,
da ich sie aufgab und von schwärzlichem Mitternachtshonig lebe
hinter meinen flüssiggewordenen Augen.

V

Ich habe sie nicht gerufen, aber sie verfinstern meine Stimme.
Doch jeder soll wissen, daß ich verlernt habe zu beten,
denn ich bin verkommen an einem Augusttag
                    des Jahres 1952,
jeder soll wissen, daß ich erstickt bin in meinem Fleisch.

VI

Niemand hört meine Stimme, die mich vernichten wird.
Sie werden mein Haus umzingeln und meine Tür
                    eintreten und den Namen rufen,
auf den ich höre.
Sie werden vergessen, daß auch ich der Schöpfer des Grases
und der Erhalter der Milch und des Honigs bin. –
In einem Winkel der Traurigkeit werden sie mich erschlagen,
wenn Schnee und Wind und Frühling zu spät kommen . . .

IV

I eat my bread at a window seat and
gaze into her face, which looks like the flesh of a lion
and of destruction.
I see her brain drip onto the debauched
                              carpet of country villages,
which have never drunk as much pain as these days,
because I have forsaken them and live now from the
                              blackish midnight honey
behind my liquefied eyes.

V

I have not called them, but they darken my voice.
Yet each one should know that I have forgotten how to pray,
since I became debauched on an August day
                              in the year 1952,
each one should know that I have suffocated within my own flesh.

VI

No one hears this voice of mine, which will destroy me.
They will surround my house and kick in the door
                              and call the name
to which I answer.
They will forget that I, too, am the creator of the grass
and the sustainer of the milk and the honey.—
In a corner of the sadness they will kill me,
if snow and wind and spring come too late . . .

Ein Abend

Ein Abend, an dem die Balken heruntergelassen sind,
   hinter denen sich Berge von Fleisch und Früchten,
   die Kontinente zu Staub zerfallener Seelen türmen,
ein Abend zwischen den schwarzen Bäumen des Parks
   und den müden Stößen der Magistratskapellen
   auf dem gefrorenen Asphalt zerschundener Sommer,
                              die keinen Atemzug
      deiner Herrlichkeit wiederholen,
ein Abend schwirrender Vögel und schweigsamer Bettler
   auf der Seite des weißen Parlaments, wo sie dich
                        einmal ermorden wollten,
      weil du »Vaterland« schriest und ihre Gesichter zu
                        wenig verachtetest,
ein Abend, der so kalt ist wie die Nacht vor dem Dorf
   zwischen den Baumstämmen, die den Schnee im
                        Genick haben,
ein Abend verschlossener Milchtrinkstuben, deren glatte
                        Tischplatten
      einen verzweifelten Kampf gegen den Gitarrenwirbel
                        unserer Landsleute führen,
   geschlossene Kirchen, geschlossene Bordelle,
                        geschlossene Herzen,
ein Abend unter den Kolporteuren, die unsre traurige
                        Welt in die Senkgruben schleudern:
   «Weiße! Neger! Bankherren! Totgeborgene Bergleute!
   Maschinerien! Die verstümmelten Glocken der
                        Kriegsschauplätze . . .»,
      die unser Hirn betäuben,
ein Abend, der aus der Nacht tropft und von grünen,
                        scheiternden Hängen schwärmt,
      von Kartoffelfuhrwerken,
ein Abend, der dich hineintreibt in die Verlassenheit,
   unter die schwachen Glieder,
   in die blinden Spiele des Schmerzes,
      wo zu den Lastern der Hunger den Takt schlägt . . .

An Evening

An evening on which the shutters are lowered
    and behind them tower mountains of meat and fruit,
    continents of souls crumbled to dust,
an evening between the black trees of the park
    and the tired bursts of municipal bands
    on the frozen asphalt of chafed summers,
                    which do not repeat
    a single breath of your magnificence,
an evening of whirring birds and taciturn beggars
    at the side of the white parliament, where once they
                 sought to murder you
    for screaming "Fatherland" and scorning their faces
                     too little,
an evening as cold as the night outside the village,
    between tree-trunks whose napes are draped
                     with snow,
an evening of shuttered milk bars, whose smooth
                   table tops
    fight a desperate battle against our compatriots'
                 vortex of guitars,
    closed churches, closed brothels,
                  closed hearts,
an evening among the news vendors, who speed our
              sad world's descent to the drains:
    "Whites! Blacks! Bankers! Miners Recovered Dead!
    Machinery! The mutilated bells of theaters of war . . ."
    which numb our brains,
an evening which drips from the night and gushes over
                 failing green slopes
    and potato carts,
an evening which drives you to desolation
    beneath weak limbs,
    to the blind games of pain,
    where hunger beats time to the vices . . .

Unter dem klagenden Mond

Ihr sagt nichts, weil ihr zu krank seid, zu sagen,
$\qquad\qquad\qquad\qquad\qquad$ wie stark
$\quad$ die Erde ist, die ich erschaffen habe in meinen Nächten,
die Erde des Fleisches und die Erde
$\quad$ der Sonnenlandschaften,
die Erde, die keinen Tropfen Bluts vergeudet,
$\quad$ die Erde, die meinen Vätern noch nicht geläufig war und die
mit neuen Instrumenten zu meiner Botschaft wird,
$\quad$ wenn der Sommer kommt mit dem heißen August
und der Winter mit dem Röhren der Baumstämme
$\quad$ zwischen den Bergen dieses Landstriches,
der keines zweiten Gottes würdig ist und von Brot
$\qquad\qquad\qquad\qquad\qquad$ und Eitelkeit lebt
$\quad$ seit dem Tage, an dem die Kriege erfunden wurden
in einem zerstörten Gehirn der Hauptstadt.

Ihr sagt nichts, weil ihr zu krank seid, zu sagen, wie groß
$\quad$ die Qual ist, die meine Seele durchfurchen mußte
vom Abend zum Morgen und durch die Mitternächte,
$\qquad\qquad\qquad$ die keinen Grashalm mehr spüren,
$\quad$ weil ihre Musik zu eitel ist
für die Buttertröge und die Truhen der Toten, die heraufsteigen
$\quad$ aus ihren Kerkern mit dem Quacken der Frösche
zwischen den Zeiten der Zeugungen.

Ihr sagt nichts, weil ihr zu krank seid, zu sagen, wie tief
$\quad$ das Meer ist, das mein Schiff befuhr, wie schwarz die Rücken
der Delphine glänzen an den Riffen des Traums,
$\quad$ der von tausend Gesichtern des Nordens
zu tausend Gesichtern des Südens reicht,
$\quad$ der größer ist als diese Erde und gewaltiger

Beneath the Lamenting Moon

You all say nothing, because you are too sick to say
                                        how strong
   the earth is which I created in my nights,
the earth of the flesh, the earth
   of solar landscapes,
the earth which squanders not a single drop of blood,
   the earth which once was not familiar to my fathers,
but with new instruments shall be my message,
   when summer comes with the heat of August,
and winter with its tubular tree trunks
   between the mountains of this swath of land
which merits no second God and has lived from bread
                                        and vanity
   ever since the day that wars were invented
by a ruined brain in the capital.

You all say nothing, because you are too sick to say how great
   the torment is which my soul had to furrow,
from evening to morning, through midnights that sense
                                 not even a blade of grass
   because their music is too vain
for butter vats and the chests of the dead who rise
   from their dungeons to the croaking of frogs
between times of conception.

You all say nothing, because you are too sick to say how deep
   the ocean is which my ship sailed, how black the backs
of dolphins shine on the reefs of the dream,
   which reaches from the thousand faces of the north
to the thousand faces of the south,
   which is greater than this earth and mightier

als der Novembersturm, der meinen Vätern das Leben kostete
    und Abermillionen Fuhrwerke von Tagen!
Ihr sagt nichts, weil euer Gebot mißverstanden ist
    und weil euer Fleisch vor süßer Fäulnis glänzt in der Nacht
und eure Seele durch bläuliche Wälder huscht
    in der Zeit der Kartoffeltriebe und Maiprozessionen!
Ihr sagt nichts, weil ihr zu krank seid, zu sagen, wer
    eure Verdammnis erträumt hat in den von Gott
                                erschaffenen Kerkern,
in den Gebirgshütten und Vorstadtgasthäusern, in den
                                Kellergewölben,
    deren Ratten wie Sterne funkeln,
weil Tag und Nacht die Musik des Gerölls sind,
    das euren Schlaf trinkt
und die Eroberung der Kriege,
    die ihr erfunden habt in den Frühjahrsräuschen!

Ihr sagt nichts, weil ihr zu krank seid, zu sagen, was
    gesagt werden muß, was diese Hügel so traurig macht
und diesen Sonnenaufgang und diese Mühsal der Bauern
    und diese Mühsal der Vögel
und diese Mühsal, die in jedem Halm Zerstörung
                                züchtet, in jedem Flußbett,
    überall, wo die Hände über der Erde sind.

than the November storm that cost my fathers their lives
    and millions upon millions of wagons of days!
You all say nothing, because your commandment is mistaken
    and your flesh radiates sweet decay in the night
and your soul darts through bluish woods
    in the season of potato sprouting and May parades!
You all say nothing, because you are too sick to say who
    dreamed up your damnation in God-created dungeons,
in mountain huts and suburban inns, in cellar vaults
    whose rats twinkle like stars,
because day and night are the music of the pebbles
    that drink your sleep
and the conquest of the wars
    that you invented in the flushes of spring!

You all say nothing, because you are too sick to say what
    has to be said, thereby so saddening these hills
and this sunrise and the toil of the farmers
    and this toil of the birds
and this toil that breeds destruction in every blade of grass,
                          in every riverbed,
    wherever there are hands above the earth.

In meiner Hauptstadt

I

In meiner Hauptstadt war ich ein Tagedieb, ein Pferdeknecht
    des Ministerpräsidenten und ich sah durch die Fenster
der Hofburg und dachte, daß ich niemals residieren werde
    an einem dieser Schreibtische und niemals
eine Zigarre rauchen hinter dem blauen Samtvorhang, der schon
    Metternich die Aussicht auf die grünen Bäume verdarb.

II

Ich war getrieben von seltsamen Peitschen, von Büchern
                        und Bibelwörtern,
    und der Novemberwind entblößte meine Schenkel
und sprach zornige Psalmen in mein zerquältes
                        Ländlergehirn.
    Ich stolperte über die Vornehmheiten
dieser leblosen Kreaturen, die über den GRABEN krochen
  in schwarzen und blauen Anzügen, Zigarren wippend
und ein Geschäft abschließend mit Zement- und Essigfabriken.
    Ich stolperte über die Instrumente, die einen kränklichen Mozart
lebendig zu machen versuchten,
    und über den Schmerz, der in den Gesichtern saß,
die in die Stadtbahn geschleudert waren
    wie traurige Aschenpakete, Morast erstickter Seelen,
die von Honigbroten und Schwalbenzügen,
    von fetten Wiesen und prasselnden Osterlämmern
in gärenden Tälern träumten.
    Ich stolperte über die Kirchen, deren Knabengesang
keinen Hungrigen fütterte, deren Messen dem Treiben
                        dieses Jahrhunderts
    glichen . . . dieselben Stimmen, dieselben Trompeten-
                        stöße, dieselben
    widerwärtigen Orgelpfeifen . . .

In My Capital City

I

In my capital city I was a dawdler, a groom
    of the Prime Minister's horses, and I gazed out the windows
of the Hofburg and thought how I would never reside
    at one of these desks, and never smoke
a cigar behind the blue velvet curtain, which once
    had spoilt even Metternich's view of the green trees.

II

I was driven by strange whips, by books and the words
                                            of the Bible,
    and the November wind bared my thighs
and uttered angry psalms in my tormented
                                            bumpkin's brain.
    I stumbled over the gentilities
of those lifeless creatures who crawled over the GRABEN
    in black and blue suits, cigars bobbing,
concluding business deals for cement and vinegar factories.
    I stumbled over the instruments that a sickly Mozart
had tried to bring to life,
    and over the pain that was etched in faces
slung into the metropolitan railway system
    like sad packets of ashes, a mire of smothered souls
dreaming of slices of bread-and-honey and the passage of swallows,
    of luxuriant fields and Easter lambs
in fermenting valleys.
    I stumbled over churches, whose choirboys' voices
fed no hungry mouths, and whose services resembled
                                the goings-on of this century
    . . . the same voices, the same trumpet-blasts, the same
    repugnant piping of organs . . .

III

In meiner Hauptstadt ging ich schlafen, wenn der Tag aufstand
    mit seinem zerfurchten Gesicht und die Milchmänner
schweigsam ihr Tagwerk begannen, wenn die Kinder aufschreckten
    in ihren verweinten schmutzigen Bettgestellen
und wieder zurückfielen in die Nacht,
    die ihr junges Fleisch liegen ließ.
Ich hörte die neuen Mütter stöhnen und goldene Lampen
    sah ich im duftenden Parkwind schaukeln,
durch den mein Gehirn manchmal schwankte, wenn es zerschellt war
    in dieser Verstorbenen an der Donau.

IV

Ich war gekommen, um ihre Kerker zu sehen und ihre Arbeit,
    ihre Gesichter und ihre Einsamkeit,
ich war gekommen, weil mich vor Milch und Honig ekelte,
    vor diesen viehischen Getränken des Himmels!
Ich habe von Hochzeiten gehört, deren Tafeln
    zusammenbrechen unter der Last der Früchte und unter
dem Fest der Musik . . . Von Galaempfängen und Philosophien,
    von Bibliotheken und den Marksteinen der Römer
                     und Griechen . . .

V

Aber was fand ich in meiner Hauptstadt?
    Den Tod mit seinem Aschenmaul, vernichtend,
                     Durst und Hunger,
der meinem eignen Hunger doch zuwider war, denn es war
    ein Hunger nach Fleisch und Brot, nach Gesichtern
                     und Toiletten,
ein Hunger, der die Schande dieser Stadt lallt,
    ein Hunger nach Erbärmlichkeit,

III

In my capital city I went to bed when the day rose
    with its furrowed face, and the milkmen
began their work in silence, when children awoke in fright
    in tear-stained and dirty bedsteads
and fell back once again into the night
    which left their young flesh untouched.
I heard new mothers groan and saw golden lamps rocked
    by the sweetly scented park wind,
through which my brain sometimes swayed when shattered
    in this corpse of a city on the Danube.

IV

I had come to see its dungeons and its work,
    its faces and its loneliness,
I had come because I was nauseated by milk and honey,
    by these bestial drinks of heaven!
I had heard of weddings whose banqueting boards
    collapsed beneath the weight of fruit and beneath
the feast of music . . . Of gala receptions and philosophies,
    of libraries, and the landmarks of the Romans
                        and Greeks . . .

V

Yet what did I find in my capital city?
    Death with its ashen mouth, destructive,
                        thirst and hunger,
repugnant to my own hunger because a hunger
    for meat and bread, for faces and appearances,
a hunger which prattled the shame of this city,
    a hunger for misery,

von Fenster zu Fenster schimmernd, Frühling und
                                  faulen Ruhm erzeugend
  unter den Treppen des Himmels.
Ich war gefangen und von Fäulnis müd,
    fern der Wälder und fern der Todessüchte zerfallener
                                         Jahre.
Die grauen, zerbröckelnden Steine dieses Gebälks
                            klagten wild,
  doch ich selbst war Gelächter, Gelächter der Hölle,
das mich die Menschenfalle, in die ich gelaufen war,
  vergessen ließ, eine schwärzliche Stunde der Welt
im Novemberwind meines Daseins . . .

shimmering from window to window, bearing spring
                              and lazy glory
    beneath the staircase of the heavens.
I was caught and tired of decay,
    far from the woods and far from the death-craving
                              of moldered years.
The gray crumbling stones of this entablature
                              lamented wildly,
    yet I myself was all laughter, the laughter of hell,
which let me forget the human traps into which I had run,
    a blackish hour of the world
in the November wind of my existence . . .

Paris

Dein Weinen dem, der es nicht will.

Paul Eluard

I

Ich kann nicht schlafen, denn der Zirkus ist aufgefahren
   vor meinem Fenster und die Menschen jubeln! Wie
                    durch das Gras
der Hölle sehe ich ihre Gesichter, die dieser Stadt die
                     Vernichtung
   und die unerschöpflichen Poesien bringen, von denen ich
schlafend zwischen Nancy und Versailles gehört habe,
   von den Kerkerzellen unter den Sternen des Flusses,
der seine Bitternis in den Himmel schickt,
   an den Ufern und in den Wäldern, die von den
             Leichen der Deutschen stinken.
Ich habe geschlafen, als ich Hirte war und meine Bibel las
   und nicht an die Untergrundbahn dachte, die meinen
             Schlaf zerschnitt,
als wäre ich schuldig, als hätte ich Mädchen zerstört
   und junge Männer zu einem Schlaf durch zehn Stunden verleitet,
als wäre ich einer der Bettler, die ihr Gesicht nicht zeigen,
   wenn die Sonne über der Kathedrale spazieren geht,
als wäre ich der Mann mit den Augen, die euch erstechen,
                    denn
   ich möchte nicht verhungern, »à la fin tu es las de ce
             monde ancien . . .«
O, ich kenne meinen Pascal und meine Dichter der Pavillons,
   das Gestöhn aus den Krankenhäusern über der Seine,
das der stinkende Morgen durch dein Fenster treibt, mitten
   in dein Herz, das du tragen mußt, auch wenn du es
             verzehren möchtest
dieses Herz, auf einem grünen sonnigen Platz, dieses Herz,
   das einmal im süßen Heu kroch und von raunenden

Paris

Weep for those who do not wish you to.
Paul Eluard

I

I cannot sleep, for the circus has started up
   outside my window and people are cheering! As if
                     through the grass
of hell I see their faces, which bring this city
                      its destruction
   and the inexhaustible verses which I heard
sleeping between Nancy and Versailles,
   like the dungeon cells beneath the stars of the river
which sends its bitterness up into the sky,
   to the river banks and into the forests, which stink
                of the corpses of Germans.
I slept, as when I was a shepherd and read my Bible,
   and did not think of the underground railway slicing
                through my sleep
as if I were guilty, as if I had destroyed girls
   and enticed young men to sleep for ten hours,
as if I were one of those beggars who do not show their faces
   when the sun goes strolling across the cathedral,
as if I were the man with eyes that stab you to death,
                    because
   I do not wish to starve, "à la fin tu es las de ce
               monde ancien . . ."
O, I know my Pascal and my poets of the pavilion,
   the groaning from the hospitals across the Seine
which fetid morning propels through the windows, right
   into the middle of your heart, which you have to bear, even if
             you would rather devour
this heart, on a green and sunny square, this heart,
   which once crawled about in the sweet hay and dreamed of

Milchkübeln träumte,
dieses Herz, das auf den Landstraßen erstickte, das in
Fabriken war
und den Schweiß der stumpfsinnigen Käsereiarbeiter
einatmen mußte,
dieses Herz, das den Tag aufgehen sah, bevor die Sonne kam,
das mit Dieben auf kalten Pritschen schlummerte
am Ende der Eisenbahnzüge,
an den Ufern der Räusche,
an den Ufern des Grases,
an den Ufern des Ruhms,
an den Ufern der Wissenschaft,
dieses Herz, das hinausgehen möchte aus dem Gefängnis,
um frei zu sein wie die Vögel
und wie die Märzwolken über dem Eiffelturm, mit
dem ich allein bin,
um die größten Gespräche des Jahres zu führen,
dieses Jahres der Trauer.

II
Ich kann nicht schlafen, denn drei Millionen machen viel Lärm!
Drei Millionen, die von den Errungenschaften der
Technik träumen,
die ihren Kampf beten unter den Stößen der Lokomotiven,
die aus den gläsernen Sarkophagen zum Morgen dampfen,
ich kann nicht schlafen, denn ich weiß, sie verachten mein Gesicht,
dieses Gesicht, das einmal Fleisch und Blut war
und das sich in dieser Nacht zusammenzieht zur Fratze
des Teufels,
zum Abgrund, zum Untergang,
das keines Friedens würdig ist,
dieses mein Gesicht, das mehr sah, als alle Gesichter
dieser Stadt zusammen,

                    the murmur of milk churns,
this heart which choked on country roads, which was inside
                                        factories
    and had to inhale the sweat of stupefied cheese
                                        workers,
this heart, which saw day rise before the sun came,
    which slumbered with thieves on cold pallets
at the end of the railway trains,
        on the banks of raptures,
        on the banks of grass,
        on the banks of glory,
        on the banks of science,
this heart, which longs to leave the prison and be free
                                        like the birds
and like the March clouds above the Eiffel Tower, with
                                which I am alone,
    in order to engage in the best talks of the year,
of this year of sorrow.

II
I cannot sleep, because three million make a lot of noise!
    Three million who dream of the achievements of technology,
who tell the beads of their struggle beneath the thrust
                                of the locomotives
    which steam into the morning from their glass sarcophagi,
I cannot sleep, because I know they despise my face,
    this face which once was flesh and blood
and which in this night puckers into the grotesque face
                                of the devil,
    into the abyss, into a nemesis,
unworthy of any peace,
    this face of mine, which has seen more than all the faces
                        of the city put together,

dieser Stadt, die in den Bäumen weint und unter der Seidenrobe
der Chansonette auf dem Place de la Concorde . . .

III
Wenn ich sagen könnte, wie oft ich in dieser Nacht sterben wollte,
ohne Psalm sterben und ohne Mutter und Vater, sterben
wie das Vieh,
das zusammengetrieben zwischen den Mauern erstickt,
sterben wie ein zertretener Wurm, ohne Beistand,
sterben wie die Amsel, die vom Rad der Hochbahn
zerquetscht wird,
sterben wie die Seelen der Bäume, die ihre Geheimnisse
mit dem Wind zu den Weltmeeren schicken, wenn der
Frühling kommt, denn
»à la fin tu es las de ce monde ancien . . .«,
soviel Schmerz, soviel Körpergeruch der Menschen habe
ich niemals vorher geatmet.

IV
Ich ertrage es nicht mehr, niedriger zu sein als der Spargelverkäufer,
niedriger zu sein als die Wahrsagerin und niedriger
als der Pfarrer, der seinen Fuß an den Weihwasserkessel
von Notre Dame stößt.
Ich ertrage es nicht mehr, ärmer zu sein als der Bettler,
der meine letzten zehn Francs eingesteckt hat,
ohne mir »bonjour« zu sagen,
ärmer als die Dirnen und die Kinder, die unter den Kastanienbäumen
Eis schlecken mit den Zungen des Teufels,
die aussehen wie die Zungen dieser warmen, flimmernden,
zufälligen Welt.
Sie haben alle keinen Namen, sie heißen nicht Frühling,
nicht Sommer,

of this city which weeps in the trees and beneath the silk robe
   of the chansonnier on the Place de Concorde . . .

III

If I could say how often in this night I wanted to die,
die without psalm and without mother and father,
                              die like cattle,
which, driven together, choke between the walls,
   die like a trodden worm, without succor,
die like a blackbird squashed by the wheel of the overhead
                                  railway,
   die like the souls of the trees, which send their secrets
with the wind to the oceans when spring comes, because
   "à la fin tu es las de ce monde ancien . . .",
so much pain, and more human body odor than I have
                          ever inhaled before.

IV

I can bear no longer to be lower than the asparagus seller,
to be lower than the fortune-teller and lower
than the priest who stubs his foot on the holy water basin of
                            Notre Dame.
   I can bear no longer to be poorer than the beggar
who has tucked away my last ten Francs
   without bidding me even "bonjour",
poorer than the whores, and the children beneath the chestnut trees,
   who lick ice-creams with tongues of the devil,
which look like the tongues of this warm and flickering,
                        accidental world.
   They all have no names, they are not called Spring,
                    or Summer,

nicht Winter, sie tragen den schönen Gemeinschaftsnamen PARIS
und sind in der Nacht zu sehen mit offenen Mündern
und eingefallenen Wangen, schweigsam und röchelnd
                              vor irdischen Schmerzen,
    die ihnen die Wissenschaft beigebracht hat,
damit sie Gott anklagen können!
    Du siehst sie auf Stöckelschuhen heimwärts rudern
                              und die Luft
des brüderlichen Ozeans einsaugen,Weichen stellen
    und in Trillerpfeifen blasen,
ihre Beine auf wackeligen Samtsesseln strecken, ihr
                              Geschwür verbergen
    und kleinen Mädchen ein überliefertes Wort aus der
                              Bibel vorlesen
am Bettrand, wenn die letzten Schimmer des Tages
                    genug haben von der Sonne.

V
Und wo ist dein Freund, der dir diese Poesien
                              erklären sollte,
der dir den Braten aufspießt über deinem Teller,
        während er ein Gedicht von Baudelaire rezitiert?
    Wo ist dein Freund, der dich ans Ufer begleitet in
                              einem frischen Hemd,
mit duftenden Manschetten, sich bewegend wie die
                    jungen Herren der Loireschlösser,
    aus deren Mündern nur Worte fallen wie »Valéry,
                              Eluard, Coty,
Ile de France« oder »Notre nature est dans le mouvement . . .«?

nor Winter, they bear the beautiful communal name of PARIS
    and in the night can be seen with open mouths
and sunken cheeks, taciturn and wheezing with the
                          earthly pains
    which science has taught them
to enable them to accuse God!
    You see them rowing home on high-heeled shoes,
                    sucking in the air
of the fraternal ocean, pointing the way ahead
    and blowing whistles,
stretching out legs on wobbly velvet chairs, hiding
                      their ulcer,
    and reading to little girls from the edge of the bed
words bequeathed by the Bible, when day's last shimmers
           have had enough of the sun.

V
And where is that friend of yours who's supposed to explain
                    these verses,
who skewers the roast over your plate for you,
        while he recites a poem by Baudelaire?
    Where is that friend of yours who escorts you to the
             riverbank in a clean shirt,
with sweet-smelling cuffs, moving like the young lords
              of Loire castles,
    from whose mouths fall only words such as "Valery,
             Eluard, Coty,
Ile de France" or "Notre nature est dans le mouvement . . ."?

Wo ist dein Freund, der dir zehnmal am Tage sagt,
wie reich du bist,
und der seine Gedanken spielen läßt am Rande des Teichs,
in dem die Franzosen ihrer ruhmreichen Geschichte
ins Gesicht schlagen,
wo sie sich benehmen, als wäre die Revolution erst
gestern geschlossen worden.
Wo ist dein Freund, der deine Armut preist,
die in einem Dorf des verzweifelten, zerstückelten Österreich
erschaffen worden ist
von einer Mutter, die nur drei Klassen Volksschule besuchte
und von einem Vater, den der Nordsturm wie ein Vieh
durch die Gedärme
der skandinavischen Kälte trieb,
flüchtend vor seiner scheiternden Seele?

VI

Paris: ein Meer, das dich zugrunde richtet, ein Hauch
von Dächern, Leichenhallen, von Fabriken und Seidenröcken,
ein Hauch von schillernden Bäumen und zarten, wirbelnden
Tänzen,
der Geruch von offenen Urinquartieren, wo
verlassene Männer mit ihrem goldenen Wasser
Geschicke, die, längst vergessen, kein Herz mehr trösten,
auf kristallene
Teerwände schreiben, vom Staub gefangen und vom
Hunger der Frühe,
der aufsteht mit dem Tag, der sich unter dem Brückenbogen
die Augen auswischt.
Dies ist das Laster meines Gehirns, das von Millionen
Vokabeln zerstört ist
und von Abermillionen Tröstungen, die von den Griechen

Where is that friend of yours who tells you ten times a day
                              how wealthy you are,
     and who gives his thoughts free rein at the edge of the pond
in which the French slap their glorious history in
                              the face,
     where they behave as if the Revolution had finished only
                              yesterday.
Where is that friend of yours who praises your poverty,
     created in a village in desperate, dismembered Austria
     by a mother who only attended three classes of primary school
and a father who drove the northern storm like a beast
                              through the intestines

     of Scandinavian cold,
cursing in his failing soul?

VI
Paris: a sea which will wreck you, a breath
     of rooftops, morgues, of factories and silk skirts,
a breath of scintillating trees and tender, whirling
                              dances,
     the smell of open urinals, where desolate men write
                              with their golden water
of fates that, long since forgotten, no heart now solaces,
                              on crystal
tarred walls, imprisoned by the dust and the hunger
                              of an early morning,
which rises with the day, rubbing its eyes beneath
     the arch of the bridge.
This is the vice of my brain, destroyed by millions of words
     and millions upon millions of solaces, ranging from the Greeks

bis zu den grünen und roten Lichtern der Kreuzung reichen,
 dies ist die Stelle, wo die Erde für mich am kältesten war . . .
Ich kann nicht schlafen, niemals werde ich schlafen,
 denn immer sehe ich diesen Fluß und immer
treibt mich der Ekel dieser Bordelle, diese Schönheit,
    die zwischen den Baumstämmen
 der Avenue de Ternes hinunterstirbt . . .
Ich kann nicht schlafen, denn der Zirkus ist aufgefahren
 vor meinem Fenster und die Menschen jubeln! Ich möchte sie alle
vergessen, denn mein Hunger ist groß . . . er stößt
    mich zurück in ein Land,
 das noch niemand gesehn hat, in ein Land grüner,
     schluchzender Frühe,
in ein Land, das meinen Namen trägt,
 ein Morgen ohne Zerstörung . . .

to the green and red lights of the crossings,
    this is the spot where the earth was coldest for me . . .
I cannot sleep, I shall never sleep,
    because always I see this river, am always
driven by the nausea of these brothels, of this beauty,
                     which dies away between
    the tree trunks on the Avenue de Ternes . . .
I cannot sleep, for the circus has started up
    outside my window and people are cheering! I would like
                     to forget them all,
for I have a great hunger . . . it thrusts me back to
                     a country
    that no one has ever seen, to a country of green and
                     sobbing fruits,
to a country that bears my name,
    a morning without destruction . . .

Venedig

Aus den faulen Fischen,
aus den faulen Katzen,
unter den zerquetschten Sommerfrüchten
wächst dein Ruhm:

Maria della Salute, Ca d'Oro,
Colleoni, Palazzo Ducale . . .

Ich zähl meine Münzen auf der Treppe,
leg mir Schinken auf das trockne Brot
und erinnre mich an den Giorgione
mit den angefressenen Wolkenfetzen,
der den Titel
      »la tempesta« trägt.

Venice

From the rotting fish,
from the lazy cats,
beneath the squashed summer fruits,
your glory grows:

Maria della Salute, Ca d'Oro,
Colleoni, Palazzo Ducale . . .

I count my coins on the steps,
place my ham on the dry bread
and remember the Giorgione
with its fretful tattered clouds
bearing the title:
      "la tempesta."

Chioggia

Aus viertausend Jahren
　　kehrten wir heim,
in unseren Augen vertrocknete
　　der Lagunenwein.
Wir sahen die Schiffe verenden
　　im rostigen Abendlicht,
doch hinter den Schiffen die Kinder
　　sahen uns nicht.

　　Sie haben die Erde nie geliebt
　　　　und das Brot,
　　ihre Betten umtrauert schweigsam
　　　　der viertausendjährige Kot.

Wir sahen die Fische nicht sterben
　　und sahen soviel Qual,
wir hörten kein Stöhnen und Klagen
　　aus dem Hospital,
wir fanden die Fenster offen
　　gegen das Meer,
von den Inseln trug der Wind
　　die Schatten der Toten her . . .

　　Die Welt aber wartete draußen
　　　　hinter dem weißen Tor,
　　über die Zypressenarme
　　　　stieg ihr milchiger Rauch empor.
　　Nur die Rippen der Schiffe glänzten
　　　　unter dem Mond zurück,
　　vor den nassen Netzen bückten
　　　　die Frauen sich um das Glück.

Chioggia

We returned home
　　after four thousand years,
the wine of the lagoon
　　drying like our tears.
We saw the ships perish
　　in the rusty light of dusk,
yet beyond the ships the children
　　could not see us.

　　They never loved the earth
　　　　nor the bread,
　　4,000-year-old excrement
　　　　quietly mourned by their bed.

We saw the fish that didn't die
　　and saw so much pain,
from the hospital heard no one
　　groan or complain,
we found the window open
　　wide towards the sea,
and from the island the wind bore
　　the shadows of the dead to me . . .

　　Yet behind the white gate,
　　　　the world waited outside,
　　above the arms of the cypress
　　　　the milky smoke rose high.
　　Reflected in the moonlight,
　　　　only the ships' ribs gleamed,
　　over wet nets the women bent
　　　　to pick what they could glean.

Dort wissen sie noch zu leben
 an einem Tag im April,
und wenn sie am Vormittag sterben,
 sterben sie still
und der Markt in dem ruhmvollen Fischernest
 ist auch heute
für alle ein Fest:
 sie tragen Olivenbüsche ins Haus
und stellen den Aal
 auf weißen Tischen aus.

 Honig schleppen sie in schwarzen Krügen
  und erzählen von den Thunfischzügen,
 hinterm Mauerwerk
  am schmalen Spalt –
 mit den Katzen
  und mit den Fischen werden sie alt,
 und sie sticken ihre Schmerzen
  am Ufer in die Tücher hinein,

und ihr Abend riecht nach Fischen,
 und ihr Grabmal ist aus Stein.
Sie heben den Sand aus den Kähnen
 und liegen nachts im Boot,
und leben von der Arbeit,
 und viele sind schon tot . . .

 Aus viertausend Jahren
  kehrten wir heim,
 in unseren Augen vertrocknete
  der Lagunenwein,
 wir sahen die Schiffe verenden
  im rostigen Abendlicht,
 doch hinter den Schiffen die Kinder
  sahen uns nicht.

They still know how to live there
    on a bright April day,
and if they die in the morning air
    they die in a peaceful way,
the fishing village market is renowned
    as a place of celebration
for all, even now:
    they carry olive bushes into the house,
then, placed on white tables,
    they lay the eel out.

        They carry honey in black pitchers
            and the tuna fish catchers,
        tell tales behind the walls'
            narrow cracks—
        they grow old
            with the fish and the cats
        and their pain they embroider
            into cloths on the shore,

and their evening smells of fish
    and their grave is made of stone.
They scoop the sand from the skiff
    and lie in the boat at night,
and they all live from their work,
    and many now have died . . .

        We returned home,
            after four thousand years,
        the wine of the lagoon
            drying like our tears.
        We saw the ships perish
            in the rusty light of dusk,
        yet beyond the ships the children
            could not see us.

Unten liegt die Stadt

Unten liegt die Stadt,
    du brauchst nicht wiederkommen,
denn ihr Leichnam ist von Blüten übersät.

Morgen spricht der Fluß.
    Die Berge sind verschwommen,
doch der Frühling kommt zu spät.

Unten liegt die Stadt.
    Du merkst dir nicht die Namen.
Aus den Wäldern fließt der schwarze Wein.

Und die Nacht verstummt.
    Die kranken Vögel kamen.
Und du kehrst nur mehr in Trauer ein.

Down There Lies the Town

Down there lies the town,
   no need for you to return,
its corpse is with blossoms overlaid.

Morning says the river.
   The mountains are still blurred,
yet the spring has come too late.

Down there lies the town.
   The names you can't retain.
From the woods, black wine pours.

And the night grows quieter.
   Since the sick birds came,
you enter only to mourn.

DIE NACHT, DIE DURCH MEIN HERZ STÖSST

✳

THE NIGHT THAT STABS
MY HEART QUITE THROUGH

Traurigkeit

Rot sind die Berge und meine Brüder gehen in meinem Hirn,
als wäre Jesus nicht gekreuzigt worden unter den Sternen,
die keine Angst haben vor den Grausamkeiten meiner Seele, die ich
in einem Tal vergraben habe, als ich noch nicht geboren war, damals,
im April, dem zornigen Monat, der die Steine wäscht
zu Grabmälern, auf denen die Gefährtinnen meiner
                                        Einsamkeit hocken,
mit blassen Gesichtern, und der Sturm ihre Augen auskratzt
unter dem fernen Mond.

Wozu diese Tage, wozu das Sterben,
wozu das alles, was ich nicht liebe, nicht den Strauch
und nicht die Blüten im Maul des Esels und nicht den Schrei
meiner Glieder im Herbst und nicht die Mühsal der Bauern
und keinen Ruhm des Schmerzes, den mir meine Mutter
                        aufbürdete, als sie sterben mußte
unter den vollgesoffenen Bräuherren am Rand des Sees, der
                                        meine Toten auffrißt
unter dem Gelächter der Sterne.

Ich habe nichts getan, das eurer Seligkeit schaden könnte, nichts,
als ein paar Verse geschrieben, die meinen Bruder zum
                                        Weinen brachten
und meine Schwester – mit den Blüten des Märzwinds
                        – zur Eifersucht, nichts gegessen,
das euch fehlte auf dem Tisch, nichts getrunken, das
                        nach euren Hochzeiten riecht und
nach dem Bänkelgesang der Kornkammern, in die ich
                        nicht mehr zurückkehren kann, weil

Sadness

The mountains are red and my brothers walk inside my brain,
as if Jesus had never been crucified beneath these stars,
which do not fear the cruelties of this soul of mine.
I buried it in a valley before even being born, way back
in an April, the angry month, when stones are washed
to sepulchers, and there my solitude's companionesses
                                        crouch,
their faces pale and the storm scratching out their eyes
beneath the distant moon.

What are these days for, what is dying for,
what is it all for, all this that I do not love, neither the shrub
nor the blossoms in the donkey's muzzle, neither the scream
of my limbs in autumn nor the toil of the farmers,
and not the glory of the pain my mother burdened me with, when
                                        she went to her death
in the pay of sozzled brewers on the edge of the lake that
                                        devours my dead
beneath the laughter of the stars.

I did nothing that might have harmed your bliss, nothing,
other than write a few verses that made my brother cry
and my sister—with the blossoms of the March wind—jealous,
                                        I ate nothing
that you lacked at table, drank nothing that bore the scent
                                        of your wedding or
smelt of bench songs in corn barns, to which I can never
                                        return, since

ich die falsche Glocke geläutet habe am Ufer des
Flusses, der meiner Trauer
die leeren Schädel der Unsterblichkeit entgegenträgt,
jeden Tag, von Morgen zu Morgen, lautlos, als wäre ich
zu Asche zerfallen, ehe
ich aufwachte im Frühlingsfleisch dieser Städte.

Woran denke ich, wenn ich die leeren Gassen sehe, die
Fenster der Männer und Frauen,
die soviel Verwesung getrunken haben, daß dich Gott schützen muß,
die dein Grün zerschnitten und dein Grau und das
Schwarz der Flüsse,
die deinen Hunger nicht rühmten und keine Traurigkeit deiner
Nächte,
in denen du mit jedem Stein und mit jedem Lurch hinunterstarbst
in Vergessenheit! In die Vergessenheit! In die Verzweiflung
der Wurzeln!

Ich sehe kein Gesicht mehr, das ich lieben könnte, kein Fleisch,
das meiner Sehnsucht Genuß brächte und keinen Tod,
der meinem Alleinsein genügte . . . Die Äcker sind leer! Die Häuser
sind violett von Kerzen! Die Türen knarren ihre Verachtung in deine
Mühsal, wenn
du heimkommst, und jeder verkommene Mund, der ein Feld besitzt,
einen Apfelbaum, eine Milchkuh, einen Rasen,
verflucht dich . . .

ringing the wrong bell on the bank of the river which carries
immortality's empty skulls down to meet my sorrow
each day, from morning to morning, soundlessly, as if I had crumbled
                                        to ashes, before
awaking in the spring flesh of these towns.

What do I think, on seeing the empty alleys, and the windows of men
                                        and women
who have drunk so much decay that God must protect you,
who cut your green and cut your gray, and the black of the rivers too,
who glorified not your hunger, nor the sadness of the nights
when you died, falling with every stone and every amphibian
into oblivion! To oblivion! Down to the despair
of the roots!

No longer do I see a single face that I could love, no flesh
that might delight my desire and no death
that would satisfy my solitude . . . The fields are empty! The houses
violet with candles! The doors slam their scorn in the face
                                        of your toil, whenever
you come home, and every decadent mouth which owns a field,
an apple tree, a milk cow, or a lawn,
curses you . . .

Und wenn du fortreisen willst, weißt du nicht, wohin!
Und wenn du Wasser trinken willst, stehst du in der Wüste!
Und wenn du betteln willst, hat dich der Schmutz
                              ihres Reichtums erwürgt!
Und wenn du dein Grab suchst, bringen sie dir eine
                              Schüssel voll Schönheit!

. . . Ich sehe kein Gesicht mehr . . . Nur den schwarzen,
                              zerfallenden Lehm
ihrer Gebrechen und den Zorn, der ihr Leben verwandelt
                              zu Staub.

And when you wish to travel, you do not know where to!
And when you wish to drink water, you are standing in the desert!
And when you wish to beg, the dirt of their wealth chokes you
                                                    to death!
And when you visit your grave, they bring you a bowl full
                                        of beauty!

. . . No longer do I see a single face . . . Only the black
                                        crumbling clay
of their frailty, and the anger which transforms their life
                                        into dust.

Biographie des Schmerzes

Wo ich gestern geschlafen habe, ist heute Ruhetag. Vor dem Eingang
stehen die Stühle übereinander und keiner, den ich nach mir
frage, hat mich gesehen.
Die Vögel sind aufgeflattert, um mein Gesicht in die Wolken
zu zeichnen über meinem Haus und über dem Garten der Toten.

Ich habe mit den Toten gesprochen und von der Gitarre der Welt
geredet, die ihre Münder nicht mehr erzeugen und ihre Lippen,
die eine Sprache sprechen, die den Hund meines Vetters kränkt.

Die Erde spricht eine Sprache, die keiner versteht,
denn sie ist unerschöpflich – ich habe Sterne und Eiter aus ihr gerissen
in den Verzweiflungen
und Wein getrunken aus ihrem Krug,
der aus meinen Schmerzen gebrannt ist.

Diese Straßen führen in die Verbannung. Ich höre Gott
hinter einer Glasscheibe und den Teufel in einem Lautsprecher
und beide erreichen zusammen mein Herz, das den
                    Niedergang der Seelen verkündet.

Unaufhörlich wirbelt das Laub in die Gassen
und richtet Zerstörung an unter den Denkmälern.
Ich möchte im Oktober vom Grün träumen.
Unter der Haustür steht ein Gebot angeschlagen, das Gebot:
    DU SOLLST NICHT TÖTEN
– – – in der Zeitung aber stehen jeden Tag drei Morde,
die von mir sein könnten oder von einem meiner Freunde.

Biography of Pain

Where I slept yesterday, it's rest day today. In front of the entrance
the chairs stand on top of one another, no one whom I ask
about myself has seen me.
The birds have fluttered up to draw my face in the clouds
above my house and above the garden of the dead.

I have talked with the dead and spoken about the guitar of the world,
which their mouths no longer make, their lips
now speaking a language that sickens my cousin's dog.

The earth speaks a language that no one understands
because inexhaustible—I have seen stars and pus torn out of it
in fits of despair
and wine drunk from its jug
—the one which was fired from my pain.

These streets lead to banishment. I hear God
behind a pane of glass and the devil in a loudspeaker
and both together reach my heart, which announces the
                              demise of the soul.

Incessantly the leaves in the alleys whirl,
wreaking havoc beneath the monuments.
I would like to dream of greenery in October.
A commandment is fastened beneath the front door,
                              the commandment:
    THOU SHALL NOT KILL
— — — yet there are three murders a day in the papers,
any of which could have been done by me, or by one of my friends.

Ich lese sie wie eine Fabel,
von einem Messerstich zum andern – ohne, daß ich mich langweile.
Während sie Fleisch und Ruhm verwechseln, schläft meine Seele
unter der Handbewegung Gottes.

I read them like a fable,
from one stab of the knife to the next—without getting bored.
While they confuse flesh and glory, my soul sleeps
beneath the movement of God's hand.

Qual

Ich sterbe vor der Sonne und
vor dem Wind und vor den Kindern, die sich um den
                              Hund streiten, ich sterbe
an einem Morgen, der zu keinem Gedicht werden
                    kann; nur traurig und grün und endlos
ist dieser Morgen . . .Vater und Mutter stehn auf der
                                        Brücke und glauben,
ich komme aus der Stadt, und bringen mir nichts
als ihre zerfallenen Frühlinge in großen Körben und sehen mich –
und sehen mich nicht, denn
ich sterbe vor der Sonne.

Eines Tages werde ich die Büsche nicht mehr sehen, und das Gras
wird meiner Schwester Traurigkeit annehmen. Der Torbogen
wird schwarz sein und der Himmel nicht mehr
unerreichbar
für meine Verzweiflungen . . . An einem Tage werde
ich alles sehen und vielen die Augen auslöschen
in der Frühe . . .

Dann bin ich wieder unter den Jasminbüschen und
sehe dem Gärtner zu, wie er die Toten ordnet in den
                              Beeten . . .
Ich sterbe vor der Sonne. –
Ich bin traurig, weil es immer wieder Tage gibt, die nicht
                    mehr kommen . . . Nirgendwohin.

Torment

I die before the sun and
before the wind and before the children fighting about
                                    the dog, I die
on a morning which cannot become a poem; sad
                            and green and endless only
is this morning . . . father and mother stand on the bridge
                                    and believe
I am coming from the city, and so bring me nothing
but their decayed springtimes in big baskets and see me –
and do not see me, since
I die before the sun.

One day I shall no longer see the bushes, and the grass
shall take on my sister's sadness. The arch of the gate
shall be black and heaven no longer
unattainable
for my despair . . . One day I shall
see everything and extinguish the eyes of many
in the early morning . . .

Then once again I am under the jasmine bushes and
watching the gardener, how he arranges the dead in the
                                    flowerbeds . . .
I die before the sun.—
I am sad because time and again there are days which
                    do not return . . . Going nowhere.

In einen Teppich aus Wasser

In einen Teppich aus Wasser
sticke ich meine Tage,
meine Götter und meine Krankheiten.

In einen Teppich aus Grün
sticke ich meine roten Leiden,
meine blauen Morgen,
meine gelben Dörfer und Honigbrote.

In einen Teppich aus Erde
sticke ich meine Vergängnis.
Ich sticke meine Nacht hinein
und meinen Hunger,
meine Trauer
und das Kriegsschiff meiner Verzweiflungen,
das hinübergleitet in tausend Gewässer,
in die Gewässer der Unruhe,
in die Gewässer der Unsterblichkeit.

Into a Carpet Made of Water

Into a carpet made of water
I embroider my days,
my gods and my ailments.

Into a carpet made of greenery
I embroider my red pain,
my blue mornings,
my yellow villages and slices of bread-and-honey.

Into a carpet made of earth
I embroider my transience.
I embroider my night into it
and my hunger,
my sorrow
and the warship of my despair,
which glides across on a thousand waters,
to the waters of restlessness,
to the waters of immortality.

Die Nacht

Die Nacht bebt vor dem Fenster, sie will durch mein
                                  Herz stoßen
und die Namen rufen, die ich geschändet habe.
O, diese Namen, die in jedes Kreuz geschnitzt sind und
                         mein Tagwerk beschmutzen.
Ich weiß, ich werde aufstehen und mein Bett vernichten
und mit dem Bett die Träume, die in mein Haar
                          wuchsen für siebzig Jahre.

Ich werde aufstehen und meinen Vers herunter sagen
für die Bettler, die von Verlassenheit leben,
auf den Straßen der Geschäfte. Auf den Straßen,
auf denen die Frauen ihr Fleisch betrügen für einen
                          Jahrmarktstag.
Diese Straßen, die geschaffen sind aus dem Weizen meines Vaters
und aus der Armut meiner Mutter,
die sich mit einer Sense den Arm aufschnitt und dabei aussah
wie die Sonne selbst. –

O, die Nacht, die durch mein Herz stößt
mit allen, die ich geschändet habe . . .

The Night

Night shakes outside the window, seeks to pierce my heart
                                        quite through
and call the names I have defiled.
O these names, carved into every cross, sullying
                                        my day's work.
I know I shall get up and destroy my bed
and with the bed the dreams that have grown in my hair
                                        for seventy years.

I shall get up and recite my verse
for the beggars who live from desolation
on streets full of shops. On streets
where women betray their bodies for a day
                                        at the fairground.
These streets that are made from my father's wheat
and my mother's poverty,
she who cut her arm with a scythe, and then looked
just like the sun itself.—

O, the night, which pierces my heart quite through
with everything I have defiled . . .

Nichts weißt du, mein Bruder, von der Nacht

Nichts weißt du, mein Bruder, von der Nacht,
nichts von dieser Qual, die mich erschöpfte,
gleich der Poesie, die meine Seele trug,
nichts von diesen tausend Dämmerungen, tausend Spiegeln,
die mich stürzen werden in den Abgrund.
Nichts weißt du, mein Bruder, von der Nacht,
die ich wie den Strom durchwaten mußte,
dessen Seelen längst erwürgt sind von den Meeren,
und du weißt nichts von dem Zauberspruch,
den mir unser Mond zwischen den dürren Ästen
öffnete wie eines Frühlings Frucht.
Nichts weißt du, mein Bruder, von der Nacht,
die mich trieb durch meines Vaters Gräber,
die mich trieb durch Wälder, größer als die Erde,
die mich lehrte Sonnen auf- und niedergehn zu sehen
in den kranken Finsternissen meines Tagwerks.
Nichts weißt du, mein Bruder, von der Nacht,
von der Unruh, die den Mörtel plagte,
nichts von Shakespeare und dem blanken Schädel,
der wie Stein millionenfache Asche trug,
der hinunterrollte an die weißen Küsten,
über Krieg und Fäulnis mit Gelächter.
Nichts weißt du, mein Bruder, von der Nacht,
denn dein Schlaf ging durch die müden Stämme
dieses Herbstes, durch den Wind, der deine Füße wusch
                                        wie Schnee.

Nothing Do You Know, My Brother, of the Night

Nothing do you know, my brother, of the night,
nothing of this torment which exhausts me,
like the poetry that bore my soul,
nothing of these thousands of twilights, thousands of mirrors
that will plunge me into the abyss.
Nothing do you know, my brother, of the night,
that I had to wade through, like the current of a stream
whose souls were long since strangled by the seas,
and nothing do you know of the magic charm
which once opened up our moon for me,
like a spring fruit between the dry branches.
Nothing do you know, my brother, of the night,
which drove me through my father's graves,
which drove me through forests greater than the earth,
which taught me to see the suns rise and set
in the sick eclipses of my day's work.
Nothing do you know, my brother, of the night,
of the anxiety that tormented mortar,
nothing of Shakespeare and the shiny skull,
which, like stone, bore ashes millionfold,
and rolled its way down to the white coasts,
over war and putrefaction, with laughter.
Nothing do you know, my brother, of the night,
for your sleep has passed through the tired tree trunks
of this autumn, and through the wind which washed
your feet like snow.

Was treibt die Seelen
durch die Fliederbüsche

Was treibt die Seelen durch die Fliederbüsche,
den Wind aus den Wäldern, der seine Sprüche über die weiße
Fläche des Sees treibt, der die Gesichter jahrhundertealten Schmerzes
in die Kerkerzelle der Bauern und Mönche meißelt,
wo Tausende sterben und die Musik der Vögel besitzen
für ihre Errungenschaften und den lautlosen Gang
verstorbener Tiere, die in das Dunkel des Bergwerks fliehen,
die Welt zu verwandeln in eine vom Regen zerpeitschte Hölle?

Was treibt die Seelen durch die Fliederbüsche
an diesem Morgen, wo kein Haus mehr zu sich selbst findet
und keiner der Gärten leuchtet von den Marksteinen der Poesie,
wo des greisen Maurers Mörtel verrinnt vor den Wäldern,
die diese Öde umgrenzen für eine Zeit, die nicht mehr unsere ist?
Sie finden keine Kieselsteine mehr für ihre Qual
und für die Qual des Vaters und der Mutter.
Ihre Schwester wird sie anschaun eines Morgens
mit den Augen der Nacht . . .

Was treibt die Seelen durch die Fliederbüsche,
die diese grausame Erde verzaubern um Acht, wenn
                              der Leichentransport
mit der Wöchnerin unter Zedern und Pappeln
über den weißen, knisternden Kies in den Himmel
                    fährt . . . und Minuten später
die Kinder mit ihren Schulranzen herausstürzen aus den Türen
und die grüne Erde bevölkern mit Geschrei,
das die Toten aufweckt und die alten Spitalswärter
                              während des Frühstücks
Schimpfbrocken gegen den Frühling ausstoßen läßt . . .?

What Drives the Souls
through the Lilac Bushes

What is it that drives the souls through the lilac bushes
and the wind from the woods, drives its sayings across the white
surface of the lake, chisels the faces of the pain of centuries
into the dungeon cells of farmers and monks,
where thousands die, possessing for their attainments
the music of birds and the silent step
of dead animals fleeing to the darkness of the mine,
to transform the world into a rain-lashed hell?

What is it that drives the souls through the lilac bushes
on this morning where no house finds itself any more,
and none of the gardens shine with landmarks of poetry,
where the aged mason's mortar trickles away at the edge of the forest
which surrounds this wasteland for a time, a time no longer ours?
Now they find not even pebbles for their torment
and for the torment of their fathers and mothers.
Their sister will look at them one morning
with the eyes of the night . . .

What is it that drives the souls through these lilac bushes
which enchant this cruel earth at eight, when the hearse
with the woman in childbirth passes beneath cedars and poplars,
over white, crackling gravel, and ascends to heaven . . .
                                        and minutes later
children tumble from doors with their school satchels,
populating the green earth with their cries,
waking the dead and making the old hospital porters utter
snatches of oaths against spring during breakfast . . .?

Was treibt die Seelen durch die Fliederbüsche,
wenn der Nebel des Bluts durch die Gärten steigt
und die Hänge schwer atmen unter dem grünen
                              Fleisch des erwachenden Tages,
dessen Trübsal träg in den Fluß strömt mit sanften Klagen,
wo die Mädchen des Lyzeums ihre schwarzen Röcke
und die weißen Schleifen im Haarzopf hassen
und stumm hinter dem erstickten Geist der Nonnen ins
                              Erdreich treten
immer höher auf den Hügel, zur Kapelle,
einen alten Psalm zu singen?

Was treibt die Seelen durch die Fliederbüsche,
den Schrei, der dem Schlaf entfloh, die Silben der Finsternis,
die Krankheit und den Durst der heimlichen Umbringer,
die den Traum erwürgen zwischen den Apfelbäumen
und den fernen Schatten der Stadt,
die der Tod schlägt mit den Schatten des Frühlings,
die ihren Taumel liebt mit tausend gespenstischen Sonnen,
mit Millionen Mündern und Augen, die in Feuer aufgehen,
in das ergreifende Schauspiel des Nichts, wenn das
                              Geschwür des Tages
die Gedanken an Birnen und Flüsse, an Kinder und
                              Greise, die betrübt sind, zudeckt?

What is that drives souls through the lilac bushes,
when the mist of the blood ascends through the gardens
and the slopes breathe heavily beneath the green flesh
                                        of waking day,
whose misery flows with soft laments, lethargically into the river,
where grammar school girls hate their black skirts
and the white ribbons in their braided hair,
and enter the earthly realm in silence, behind the suffocated
                                        spirit of the nuns,
climbing ever higher up the hill to the chapel
to sing an old psalm?

What is it that drives the souls through the lilac bushes,
the cry which escaped from sleep, the syllables of darkness,
the sickness and thirst of secret killers
who strangle the dream between the apple trees,
and the distant shadows of the city
which death casts with the shadows of spring,
and which loves their frenzy with a thousand ghostly suns,
with millions of mouths and eyes going up in the fire,
in the gripping play of nothingness, when the ulcer of day
covers the thoughts of pears and rivers, of children
                                        and the gloomy aged?

Erschütterung

Ich werde hinüber gehen und schreien, laut schreien
und meinen Vater rufen und ein Geständnis vorbringen,
aufstehn im Feuer und meine brennenden Hände
in den Rachen des Schnees stecken.

Ich werde die Blumen heimjagen von den Feldern
und meinen Büschen die Äste brechen für die
                                        Erschütterung des Todes.
Ich werde meiner Trauer einen Brief mitgeben und sie
                              Gott empfehlen
und ihr sagen, daß sie Leben ist wie keine Leben,
Trauer in der Dämmerung der Vaterstädte!

Ich werde hinüber gehen und verkünden, woher ich gekommen bin
und wohin ich gehe.
Ich gehe so weit, bis mich keiner mehr einholen kann
mit schmutzigen Schuhen. Kein Frost wird mein Herz versteinern
vor der Ungewißheit der trüben Götter!

Convulsion

I shall walk over and shout, shout loudly
and call my father and make a confession,
arise in the fire and thrust my burning hands
into the throat of the snow.

I shall chase the flowers back home from the fields
and break the boughs of my bushes for the
                                    convulsion of death.
I shall give my sorrow a letter to deliver and
                                  commend it to God,
telling it how it is a life like no life,
sorrow in the twilight of my native towns.

I shall walk over and declare whence I came
and where I'm going.
I'll walk so far, till no one can catch up with me ever again
in their dirty shoes. No frost shall petrify my heart
before the uncertainty of the gloomy gods!

Vorhölle

Ich habe Dich gesehen wie einen Ertrinkenden
    mit offenem Maul
    über der Welt.
Ich habe Dich gesehen,
    aber über der Brücke steht eine Wolke, die nicht duldet,
    daß wir unser Haus verkaufen und unser Herz verbrennen
    für einen Jahrmarktstag und zusehen, wie der Rabe
                           sein Fleisch frißt,
    und die Kuh ihren eigenen Schmutz zerstampft.
Ich habe Dich gesehen,
    Dein Gesicht ist das Gesicht der Hölle.
Ich habe Dich gesehen,
    Deine Füße gehen durch meine Wälder und stiften Qual.
    Deine Stimme flüchtet durch meine Zimmer.
Ich habe Dich gesehen,
    Dein Blut macht mich krank: mein Haar zerfällt
                        unter der Erde,
    unter der wunderbaren Erde,
    die nach dem Gras verhängnisvoller Steppen riecht.

Limbo

I have seen you like someone drowning,
   your mouth open
   above the world.
I have seen you,
   yet above the bridge is a cloud which does not accept
   that we sell our house and burn our heart
   for a day at the fairground, and watch how the raven
                             devours its meat
   and the cow tramples its own dirt.
I have seen you,
   your face is the face of hell.
I have seen you,
   your feet pass through my forests, causing torment.
   your voice flees through my room
I have seen you,
   your blood makes me sick: my hair crumbles
                          beneath the earth,
   beneath the marvelous earth,
   which smells of the grass of ominous steppes.

Aschermittwoch

Ich möchte hinausgehen
    nach der Nacht,
und meine Hände und meine Lippen
    reinigen,
ich möchte mich reinigen
    an der Sonne und
an den Gräsern –

    Aber es regnet,
und meine Gräser
    sind braun
und alt –

Ash Wednesday

I should like to go out
    to the night,
and clean my hands
    and my lips,
I should like to clean myself
    with the sun and
with the grass—

    But it's raining,
and my grass
    is brown
and old—

Neun Psalmen

I

Ich will zornig sein,
ich will alles vergessen,
ich will das Maul der Fische vergessen,
denn das Maul der Fische ist finster.
Ich will meinen Kampf beten,
den großen Kampf um meine Seele.
Denn ich bin arm.
In der Nacht bin ich bettelarm.
Alle haben mich vergessen,
aber ich sehe den Tisch
und den Wein, den ich trinken werde.
Es ist der Wein Gottes,
der schwarze Wein für mein rotes Hirn,
den ich trinken werde in der Nacht,
in der Nacht, die meine Füße verbrennt,
die mein Land und die Meere verschüttet,
die Nacht der Betrogenen,
die Nacht der glühenden Apfelbäume,
die Nacht der Brunnen,
die Nacht der Bänkelsänger,
die Nacht, die meine Schlangenköpfe zerstampft,
die Nacht der Gescheiterten,
die Nacht der Fische.
Ich werde ihn trinken.
Ich will ihn zornig trinken
in der Nacht meiner völligen Armut.

II

Jede Nacht führt mein Weg in die Schottergrube,
in die Schottergrube meiner Verzweiflungen,
in das Geröll,
in die Bitternis,
die meine Augen ohnmächtig macht.

Nine Psalms

("God's soul is in the fishes")

I

I want to be angry,
I want to forget everything,
I want to forget the fishes' mouth
for the fishes' mouth is dark.
I want tell the beads of my struggle,
the great struggle for my soul.
For I am poor.
In the night I am poor as a beggar.
All have forgotten me,
but I see the table
and the wine, which I shall drink.
It is God's wine,
black wine for my red brain,
and I shall it drink in the night,
in the night that burns my feet,
which convulses my land and the seas,
the night of the betrayed,
the night of glowing apple trees,
the night of the wells,
the night of the wandering minstrels,
the night which tramples my serpent-heads,
the night of those who failed,
the night of the fishes.
I shall drink it.
I shall drink it angrily
in the night of my complete poverty.

II

Every night my path leads me to the gravel pit,
to the gravel pit of my despair,
to the pebbles,
to the bitterness
which renders my eyes powerless.

Ich höre in den Steinen
die Wut der Winde,
die meine armseligen Kinder zerstäubt.
Herr,
mein verwunschener Name,
der verwunschene Name meiner Kinder
stöhnt in den Steinen!
Du aber bist der unaufhörliche Regen der Trauer,
der unaufhörliche Regen der Verlassenheit,
der Regen der Sterne.
Der Regen der Schwachen,
der meine Augen ohnmächtig macht.

III
Was ich tue, ist schlecht getan,
was ich singe, ist schlecht gesungen,
darum hast Du ein Recht
auf meine Hände
und auf meine Stimme.
Ich werde arbeiten nach meinen Kräften.
Ich verspreche Dir die Ernte.
Ich werde singen den Gesang der untergegangenen Völker.
Ich werde mein Volk singen.
Ich werde lieben.
Auch die Verbrecher!
Mit den Verbrechern und mit den Unbeschützten
werde ich eine neue Heimat gründen –
Trotzdem ist, was ich tue, schlecht getan,
was ich singe, schlecht gesungen.
Darum hast du ein Recht
auf meine Hände
und auf meine Stimme.

IV
Ich werde an den Rand gehn,
an den Rand der Erde
und die Ewigkeit schmecken.

I hear in the stones
the anger of the winds
which scatters my wretched children.
Lord,
my haunted name,
the haunted name of my children
groans in the stones!
Yet you are the incessant rain of sorrow,
the incessant rain of desolation,
the rain of the stars.
The rain of the weak,
which renders my eyes powerless.

III
What I do is done badly,
what I sing is sung badly,
which is why you have a right
to my hands
and to my voice.
I shall work according to my powers.
I promise you the harvest.
I shall sing the song of perished peoples.
I shall sing of my people.
I shall love.
Even the villains!
With the villains and with the vulnerable
I shall found a new homeland—
Nonetheless what I do is done badly,
what I sing is sung badly.
Which is why you have a right
to my hands
and to my voice.

IV
I shall walk to the edge,
to the edge of the Earth
and taste eternity.

Ich werde die Hände anfüllen mit Erde
und meine Wörter sprechen,
die Wörter, die zu Stein werden auf meiner Zunge,
um Gott wieder aufzubauen,
den großen Gott,
den alleinigen Gott,
den Vater meiner Kinder,
am Rand der Erde,
den uralten Vater,
am Rand der Erde,
im Namen meiner Kinder.

V

Alle Fische des Meeres
und alle Kinder der Erde
laß mich erkennen
und den Geruch des Morgens schmecken
und den Geruch des Abends.
Ich will die Sprache der Fische hören
und die Sprache des Windes,
die der Sprache der Engel gleicht.
Ich will die Stimme
der Vergängnis hören!
Alle Stimmen sind die Stimmen der Vergängnis.
Alle Stimmen, die jemals vernommen wurden.
Alle singen Vergängnis.
Auch Du singst Vergängnis.

VI

Der Abend schickt mir das Korn der Gräber,
den samtenen Geschmack der Ruhe
und den Tau der Bettelschaften.
O, diese Bettelschaften der Erde!
Ich sehe sie übers Gras gehen
in die Weihnacht der Tümpel,
in den Frühling der Gebete.

I shall fill my hands with earth
and speak my words,
the words that turn to stone on my tongue,
to build God up again,
the great God,
the sole God,
the father of my children,
at the edge of the Earth,
the primeval father,
at the edge of the Earth,
in the name of my children.

V

All the fish in the sea
and all the children on Earth,
let me know them,
and taste the smell of the morning
and the smell of the evening.
I want to hear the language of the fish
and the language of the wind,
which resembles the language of the angels.
I want to hear the voice
of transience!
All voices are the voices of transience.
All voices that have ever been heard.
All sing of transience.
You too sing of transience.

VI

The evening sends me the grain of the graves,
the velvet taste of rest
and the dew of legions of beggars!
O these beggars of the Earth!
I see them walk over the grass
to the Christmas of the ponds,
to the springtime of prayers.

Laß mich diesen Frühling sehen,
die Millionen Bettelschaften der Erde,
ehe es zu spät ist!

VII

Könnte ich sagen, was gesagt werden muß,
wie mein Körper zur größten Falle meines Lebens wird,
meine Unschuld zur größten Schuld!
Könnte ich sagen, wer ich bin –
hinter den verlöteten Türen,
hinter meinem stolzen Gedächtnis,
könnte ich sagen, wie der Kampf gegen die Gesetze
(gegen die niedrigen Gesetze)
in mir vor sich geht,
wie das Feuer meines Fleisches meine Seele verbrennt,
könnte ich sagen, was ich zu sagen bestimmt bin,
die Hölle meines Blutes,
die Finsternis meiner Augen,
die Unfruchtbarkeit meiner Lieder,
zu sagen die Armut!
Die große Armut, die mich erniedrigt.
Die große Armut, die mich vollendet.
Die Armut, die mich zerspaltet
für die Vollendung!

VIII

Schwarz ist das Gras, Vater,
schwarz ist die Erde,
schwarz sind meine Gedanken,
weil ich ein armer Mensch bin.
Schwarz ist die Erde,
schwarz ist der Sonnenuntergang,
schwarz ist meine Botschaft.
Schwarz ist der Rock, der mich nicht mehr verlassen wird,
schwarz sind die Sterne meiner Überfahrt,
schwarz ist der Gedanke an mein Sterben.
Wo habe ich dieses Schwarz, dieses zungenfeindliche
                                    Schwarz entdeckt?

Let me see this springtime,
the millions of beggar-legions on Earth
before it is too late!

VII

If I could say what needs to be said,
how my body becomes the greatest trap of my life,
my innocence the greatest guilt!
If I could say who I am—
behind the soldered doors,
behind my proud memory,
if I could say how the fight against the laws
(against the base laws)
proceeds within me,
how the fire of my flesh burns up my soul,
if I could tell of what I am destined to tell,
the hell of my blood,
the darkness of my eyes,
the unfruitfulness of my songs,
tell of poverty!
The great poverty which humiliates me.
The great poverty which perfects me.
The poverty which cleaves me
for perfection!

VIII

Black is the grass, father,
black is the earth,
black are my thoughts,
because I am a poor human.
Black is the earth,
black is the sunset,
black is my message.
Black is the jacket that will no longer desert me,
black are the stars of my crossing,
black is the thought of my death.
Where did I discover this blackness, so inimical
                                        to the tongue!

IX

Ich fürchte mich nicht mehr.
Ich fürchte nicht mehr,
was kommen wird.
Mein Hunger ist ausgelöscht,
meine Qual ist ausgetrunken,
mein Sterben macht mich glücklich.
Ich trage meine Fische
auf den Berg.
In den Fischen ist alles,
was ich zurücklasse.
In den Fischen ist meine Traurigkeit, –
und mein Scheitern ist in den Fischen.
Ich werde sagen,
wie herrlich die Erde ist, wenn ich ankomme,
wie herrlich die Erde ist . . .
Ohne mich furchten zu müssen . . .
Ich erwarte,
daß mich der Herr erwartet.

IX

I am no longer afraid.
I no longer fear
what will happen.
My hunger is extinguished,
my torment is drunk up,
my death makes me glad.
I carry my fishes
up the mountain.
In the fishes there is everything
that I leave behind.
In the fishes is my sadness—
and my failure is in the fishes.
I shall tell
how magnificent the earth is, when I arrive,
how magnificent the earth is . . .
Without having to fear . . .
I expect,
that the Lord is expecting me.

TOD UND THYMIAN

※

DEATH AND THYME

Sommerregen

Hört auf, ihr Vögel,
  mich tröstet
kein Abend, über
  der Brücke fällt Regen
in meine Trauer, mich
  ändert kein Rauschen
des Sommers,
  mich hält
kein Wind wach . . .

  Morgen früh
will ich nicht unter Bäumen
  gehn,
meine Lider sind schläfrig
  nach Winter und Schnee,
ich will im Regen
  zurückgehn
zu Blättern
  und dunklen Truhen.

Hört auf, ihr Vögel, mich friert,
  mein Schatten
wächst über
  die Nacht
in die Wälder,
  dort ruhn
unter schwarzen Blüten
  die Toten,
die wandernden Toten aus.

Summer Rain

Cease, you birds,
   no evening
comforts me, above
   the bridge, rain falls
on my sorrow, no rustle
   of summer
changes me,
   no wind
keeps me awake . . .

   Tomorrow morning
I shall not walk beneath
   the trees,
my lids are sleepy
   for winter and snow,
I shall walk back
   in the rain
to leaves
   and dark chests.

Cease, you birds, I'm freezing,
   my shadow
grows over
   the night
and into the woods,
   there beneath
the black blossoms
   the dead rest,
the wandering dead.

Vor Bryants Ruhm

Ich lebte lange in den Wäldern und auf den Gräbern,
auch war ich Zeuge, als die Sonne kam zum erstenmal und lag
bei einem Mädchen schon am Waldrand, schlafend, mehr
der Erde zugekehrt als allen Sternen . . . Ich war längst dabei,
als Shakespeare starb und Bryants Ruhm
in einem faulen Tal verdorrte.

Wer rief mich in die Städte, ließ das Grauen
herauf und ins Gehirn mir steigen, mein verlassenes Herz
gebären, das ich schon vor tausend Jahren niederschlug
an einem Zaunpfahl, dem der niederträchtigen Erde, und wer trug
mich in das Land, das meines Vaters Zorn
hinnahm wie eines alten Mannes traurige Botschaft?

Oft denke ich, daß ich zu spät die Lieder sang und auch zu spät
die Morgen überging, die Steine meiner Dörfer, die meinem Geist
zuwider sind und meiner Eitelkeit! Ihr kennt sie! Hab ich nicht
vor Eitelkeit die Poesien überrannt und alle Ställe, in denen
meine Brüder brüllen, leer, voll Wahn in schönen Nächten,
die ich selbst nicht liebte?

Ich lebte längst, doch weiß ich nicht zu sagen, wo ich zuerst
mein Fleisch begrub und müden Müttern Lügen brachte,
                              kranken Schwestern
Lieder . . . Ganz ohne Traurigkeit war ich in reifen Ländern
und Meeren, kaum, daß ich mich spürte, nur den Wind,
                              den Wind als Jubel,
den meine Fäulnis brauchte, die zerfiel in tausend Jahren. –

  Nicht an einem Tag
war ich allein, so sehr war ich in Fäulnis . . . lang vor Bryants
                              Ruhm
und lang vor Shakespeare,
  nah der Erde.

Before Bryant's Glory

Long did I live in the woods and upon the graves,
and witnessed too how the sun first came and lay
with a girl sleeping at the edge of the wood, turned
more towards the earth than any star . . . Long had I been there
when Shakespeare died and Bryant's glory
withered in a lazy valley.

Who was it that called me to the towns, and let the horror
rise and reach my brain, and give birth to my deserted heart,
which I crushed, a thousand years ago already,
against a fencepost of this vile earth, and who was it that carried me
into the land which accepted my father's anger
like a old man's sad message?

I often think I sang the songs too late, and ignored too late
the mornings and the stones of my villages, which are abhorrent
to my spirit and to my vanity—which you all know so well! Did I not,
in my vanity, overrun poetry and all the stables where
my brothers roar, vacuous and quite mad, in the beautiful nights
which I myself did not love?

I lived long ago, yet enough said about where I first
buried my flesh, brought lies to tired mothers and songs to
                                        sick sisters
. . . I was quite without sadness crossing mellow countries
and seas, hardly sensing myself at all, only the wind, the wind
                                        as the exultation
which my decay needed and which crumbled in a thousand years.—

    Not one day
was I alone, so advanced was my decay . . . long before Bryant's
                                        glory
and long before Shakespeare,
    close to the earth.

Schwarze Hügel

Ich war, denn jeder lebt nur einmal, in Italien,
Frankreich hab ich gesehn, die Terrasse des Fürsten in der Provence,
berühmte Bilder und verschlossene Seen
und die ungeheure Anstrengung im Leben
der Bauern auf den Hängen Dalmatiens; auch
das Schicksal der Strickerin auf den Stufen der Alipascha-
                            Moschee in Sarajewo
ist mir nicht fremd; Wein, Oliven, der faule Stank des Schiffsbauchs
betäubten mich, auch
trieb ich den Esel und aß den Käse, den man mit einem
                            flachen Stein zerreiben muß.
Die Kinder fütterte ich auf der Rialtobrücke. Kam ich
zu einem Sterben, wurde mein Lied nicht besiegt, noch
die Fäulnis meiner Gedanken erhöht.
Ich trank mit zerstörten Fischern und nahm
teil an ihren Festen;
der Tag zog sich zurück und schrieb
auf schwarze Hügel sein Gebrechen, daß mich fröstelte.

Selten hatte ich Heimweh in letzter Zeit, mich
rührten weder Menschen noch Türme, sogar
die Wälder blieben Wälder in meinem Gedächtnis und kein Haus
hinter den Bergen ließ mich die Welt, die ich erfand,
                        als Einziger, verlassen.
  »Das Meer ist groß, auch sind die Wüsten unerschöpflich,
  und leidet sich's nicht besser fern von diesen Orten . . . ?«
Lang schon leb ich nicht mehr von meiner Schenke.
Vater, Mutter blieben nur als Tempel. Die Welt, die
ich erfand, ernährt mich,
wenn auch die Verse und die Überreste des Fleisches
von Brot und Rückkehr, Wein und Fruchtbarkeiten handeln.

Black Hills

I have been—since we all live but once—to Italy,
France I have seen, the terrace of the prince in Provence,
famous pictures and sealed lakes
and the huge effort that life is
for the farmers on the slopes of Dalmatia; nor
is the fate of the lady who knits on the steps of Ali Pasha's
                                    Mosque in Sarajevo
foreign to me; wine, olives, and the foul stink of the ship's hold
benumbed me, further
I drove a donkey and ate cheese which one has to grate
                                    with a flat stone.
I fed the children on the Rialto Bridge. When I came across
a death, my song was not vanquished, nor did the decay
of my thoughts increase.
I drank with ruined fishermen and took
part in their celebrations;
day withdrew and wrote
its affliction on black hills till it gave me the shivers.

Seldom was I homesick in recent times, stirred
neither by people nor towers, even
forests remained forests in my memory and no house
beyond the mountains made me abandon the world that I alone
                                    invented.
   "The sea is great, and the deserts are inexhaustible
   so is it not better to suffer far away from these places . . . ?"
It is long since I lived from my tavern.
Father and mother remain only as a temple. The world which
I invented nourishes me,
albeit my verses and the remains of the flesh
treat of bread and homecoming, wine and fecundity.

Lebende und Tote

Die Seelen werden nicht wiederkommen, die der Frost
    erschütterte unter dem langsamen Gang
des Schnees, der seine Stunden
    den Geschicken nach trieb, als weckte er die Toten
am Ufer des reißenden Flusses auf.
    Morgen wird mein Vater die ersten Zweige
heimbringen von der Reise und viele werden
    seiner Traurigkeit einen Hymnus singen,
einen Hymnus von Bergen, Seen und Schatten,
    die der eiskalten Nacht entfliehen, wenn der Oktober
seine gewaltigen Verse auf die Hänge schreibt,
    von Toten und Lebenden, von der Erde,
die dem Einzelnen Ruhm bringt,
    und den Dörfern den Schmerz der Jahrtausende.
Die Seelen werden nicht wiederkommen, die der Wind
    durch die Wälder trieb nach Osten, wo meine Mutter
ihr Leben pflückte von einem verkommenen Baum,
    der keine sechsundvierzig Sommer hielt . . .
Sie werden trüb sein und keiner wird sie
    als Schwestern erkennen, keiner wird den Mond
als Vater zwischen den Stämmen nach Haus wanken sehn
    in der Mitternacht.
Sie werden von Heimweh sprechen
    und in den Hohlwegen ihrer Tage sterben, zwischen
                    dem Baumstamm
und dem Versteck der müden Amsel.
    Kein November wird kommen, wenn wir
von unseren Toten sprechen, die ihren Ruhm in der Erde
    zerfallen sehen. Morgen
wird das Meer die Toten rühmen, und dieses Jahrhundert,
    das Jahrhundert unserer Kinder,
wird vergessen sein.

The Living and the Dead

Those souls will not return which the frost
    convulsed beneath the slow progress
of the snow, which passed its hours
    in accordance with its talents, as if the dead
would wake on the bank of the racing river.
    Tomorrow my father will bring home
from his journey the first branches, and many
    will sing a hymn to his sadness,
a hymn of mountains, lakes and shadows
    fleeing the ice-cold night, when October
writes on the slopes its mighty verses
    of the dead and the living, of the earth
which brings glory to the individual,
    and the pain of millennia to the villages.
The souls will not return which the wind
    drove eastwards through the forests, where my mother
plucked her life from a rotten tree
    which lasted not forty-six summers . . .
They will be gloomy and no one will
    recognize them as sisters, no one see
the moon stagger home like a father between
    the tree trunks at midnight.
They will speak of homesickness
    and die in the ravines of their days, between the trunk
and the hiding place of the tired blackbird.
    No November will arrive when we
speak of our dead, who watch their glory decay
    in the earth. Tomorrow
the sea will glorify the dead, and this century,
    the century of our children,
will be forgotten.

Die Seelen werden nicht wiederkommen, die in den tiefen
    Dämmerungen des Herbstes in den scheiternden Tag flüchten,
in die Nacht der Kerker.
    Ein Rasen wird bleiben am Ursprung des Hügels
vor meinem Fenster, wo der Brunnenschwanz krächzt,
    der seine Geschichte verschweigt: die Geschichte
der Apfelblüten und des Todes,
    der in kalten Tagen zurückblieb,
als liebte er den Sonnenaufgang
    und die hungrigen Worte des Mühlrads, das der Nacht
und dem Strom zum Verhängnis wird.

Those souls will not return which in the deep
    twilights of fall flee to the failing day,
to the night of the dungeon.
    A lawn will remain where the hill first arose,
outside my window, where the well-handle rasps,
    concealing its story: the story
of the apple blossoms and death,
    which stayed behind in the cold days,
as if loving the sunrise
    and the hungry words of the millwheel, later to become
the downfall of the night and the river.

Mit den Schatten der Krähen

Mit den Schatten der Krähen tauchen die Toten ins Ackerland,
ein Spiel beginnend, das von Müttern handelt und von Schwestern
der traurigen Erde, die ich noch gestern im Wald und am Fluß
ihren vernichtenden Zauber sprechen hörte in der Dämmerung.

Mit den Schatten der Krähen tauchen die Toten aus dem Stolz
der grünen Berge, die meines Vaters letzte Zuflucht waren,
als der Krieg seine Marterpfähle einschlug im April,
der mit dem eisigen Wind den zarten Frühling betrübte . . .

Mit den Schatten der Krähen tauchen die Toten auf und gehen
durch die verlassenen Dörfer, die von Metzgern,
                          Pfarrern und grausamen Seelen
bevölkert sind; durch den schlammigen Friedhof, dessen Gräser
den Hymnus von der empfindsamen Erde singen, die
                        der Sonne ins rote Gesicht schlägt.

Mit den Schatten der Krähen tauchen die Toten zurück
                        in die Nacht,
den Ruhm der Bänkelsänger und Sonntagsqualen zurücklassend,
die vergessenen Steine auf dem zerfurchten Gesicht der Erde,
die in tausend Jahren durch Kirschbäume sprechen wird.

With the Shadows of Crows

With the shadows of crows the dead dive to the plowland,
beginning a game involving the mothers and sisters
of this sad earth—only yesterday, at twilight, I heard it
uttering destructive spells in the woods and by the river.

With the shadows of crows the dead emerge from the pride
of green mountains, which were my father's last refuge
when the war hammered in its martyrs' stakes in April,
afflicting gentle springtime with an icy wind.

With the shadows of crows the dead arise and walk
through deserted villages, populated by butchers, priests
and cruel souls; through the muddy graveyard, where grasses
sing the hymn of the sensitive earth that slaps the red face
                                        of the sun.

With the shadows of crows the dead dive back into the night,
leaving behind them the glory of wandering minstrels and
                                        Sunday ordeals,
and the forgotten stones on the furrowed face of the earth,
which in a thousand years will speak through its cherry trees.

Hinter den Ähren

Hinter den Ähren sterben die Krieger dieses Jahrhunderts,
das durch mein Land gezogen ist, als der April
ein Feuer für die verlorenen Seelen entzündete.
In grauen Sonnenblumen erwecke ich die Musik des Schweigens,
die meinen Errungenschaften neuen Ruhm bringt und
                                   meiner Trauer
das zerfetzte Bild der Städte, die aus Stein und Asche sind. –
Leichnam an Leichnam liegt hinter den Waffen,
die in der Morgenluft blinken vor der versinkenden Zeit.
Morgen geht mein Ruhm in die Bäche ein! Morgen erwachen
an den Rändern der Wälder die Klagen meines Fleisches, das
durch zehntausend und mehr Messer gegangen ist; der
                                   Duft der Äpfel,
die in den Pfarrhöfen dieser Landschaft faulen, dringt
unter die Musik meiner zerschundenen Schädel, die
                               keinen Frieden schicken,
bevor der Schnee hereinbricht und die Erde braun wird
von den Füßen der Verkommenen. Morgen wird mein Schweigen
die Bäume pflanzen auf neuen Hügeln, deren schwarze Gräser
in hellen Flammen aufgehen werden. Wie traurig wird dieses Land,
das mütterliche Land vor den Bergen, sein, das ich mir
                               nachkommen ließ
nach den Tagen des Meers, nach den Tagen der Fische
                       und nach den Tagen der Städte,
nach den Tafelmusiken, die die Götter der Tümpel für
                               mein Vernichtungswerk
gaben; mit Blumen und Messern und faulem Fleisch
                               und Flügelschlägen.

Behind the Ears of Corn

Behind the ears of corn they die, the warriors of this century,
which passed through my country as April
lit a fire for the lost souls.
In gray sunflowers I awaken the music of silence,
which to my attainments adds new glory, and to my sorrow
the tattered image of cities reduced to stone and ash.
Corpse upon corpse lie behind the weapons,
Which blink in the air of morning at time's descent.
Tomorrow my glory shall enter the streams! Tomorrow
at the edges of the forest, the lamentations of my flesh
                                        shall awaken,
having passed through ten thousand or more knives; the
                                      scent of apples
rotting in the rectory yards of this landscape digs its way
under the music of my chafed skulls, which send no peace
before the snow descends and the earth turns brown
beneath the feet of the depraved. Tomorrow my silence
will plant trees on new hills, whose black grasses
will burst into bright flames. How sad this land grows,
this motherly land at the foot of the mountains, which I had join me
after the days of the sea, after the days of the fishes
                           and after the days of the towns,
after the table music provided by the gods of the ponds for my
                                  work of destruction;
with flowers and knives and rotten flesh and beating of wings.

Als ich geboren wurde, war noch nicht soviel Traurigkeit in der Welt,
und die Erde war hell von den Schiffen der Geister, die
grüne Verse dichteten und in Glashäusern Träume pflanzten,
die neue Seelen verkündeten in den Freudenhäusern!
               Nicht mehr ist diese Zeit zu sehen. –
Ein elender Marktplatz spuckt seine alltäglichen Hymnen
in meine Verzweiflungen und richtet Hügel und Tote,
die durch dieses Wasser gegangen sind, durch das Wasser der Säufer,
wo sich die Gesichter treffen zu den Festen der Welt. Grau
und alt erscheinen heute die Mädchen, die uns Brot brachten
und Feuer entzündeten vor offenen Türen und die zur
               Nacht (die den Tempel erdrückte)
ihre Lieder sangen, während der Mond in den nassen
               Zweigen hing, fröstelnd, als ginge
der Schmerz der Welt bei ihm aus und ein . . . Nie wieder
kommen die frühen Ängste, nie wieder der Tag, der
               auf blauen Gesichtern blüht,
nie wieder die Nacht, die ihr Herz zerschneidet unter
               dem Kastanienbaum und
die Spalten in meinen Traum fallen läßt. Ich werde fortgehen
und die einzelnen Häuser vergessen, die Menschen
und Schweinekoben am Ufer des Sees und die schwarzen
               Spuren der Panzerfahrzeuge,
die die Felder einschnürten, das Korn, den Weizen,
dieser Menschen unwiederbringliche Lust nach dem
               Himmel! Nie wieder
erreichen mich die dumpfen Klagen des Hohlwegs und
               das Klappern der Januarhufe,
die ins Tal gleiten . . . Von den Morgen werden die
               Tautropfen fallen
und das Gewebe zersetzen, das die Laster predigt.

When I was born there was not so much sadness in the world,
and the earth was bright with the ships of the spirits, who
composed green verses and planted dreams in glasshouses,
and who announced new souls in the houses of pleasure!
                              This time is no longer to be seen!—
A miserable marketplace spits mundane anthems
into my despair and judges the hills and the dead,
who have been through this water, through the water of the drinker,
where the faces meet at the feasts of the world. Gray and old
today seem the girls who brought us bread and lit fires
in front of open doors, and at night (which smothered the temple)
sang their songs, while the moon hung in the wet branches,
                                        shivering, as if
the pain of the world went in and out of it . . . no more
shall the early fears arise, no more the day come that blooms
                              in blue faces,
no more the night which dissects its heart beneath the chestnut
                              tree and
drops the slices into my dream. I shall depart
and forget each particular house, the people
and the pigsties on the shores of the lake and the black tracks
                              of the armored vehicles
which cut into fields, into the corn and the wheat,
these human beings' irrevocable lust for heaven! No more
shall the hollow lamentations of the ravine, or the clopping
                              of January hoofs
gliding into the valley, reach me . . . dewdrops shall fall
                              from the morning
and dissolve the tissue which preaches the vices.

Einsam werden die Straßen hinunterführen in dieses
                  Leben: zu den Häßlichen!
Morgen ist alles anders! Morgen wissen die Blumen
            nichts mehr vom Abendwind! Und vom
Plätschern des Mühlwassers! Morgen ist Juni! Oder
                  November? Morgen
ist der Untergang, der zu den Inseln führt, die meiner
                Seele zugeteilt sind . . .
und meinen Gewittern!

Lonely will be the streets leading down into this life:
                              to the ugly ones!
Tomorrow everything shall be different! Tomorrow the flowers
           will know nothing of the evening wind! Or of
the plashing of the mill water! Tomorrow is June! Or
                              November? Tomorrow
is the day of doom, which leads to those islands apportioned
                              to my soul . . .

and to my storms!

Müde

Ich bin müde . . .
Mit den Bäumen führte ich Gespräche.
Mit den Schafen litt ich die Dürre.
Mit den Vögeln sang ich in Wäldern.
Ich liebte die Mädchen im Dorf.
Ich schaute hinauf zur Sonne.
Ich sah das Meer.
Ich arbeitete mit dem Töpfer.
Ich schluckte den Staub auf der Landstraße.
Ich sah die Blüten der Melancholie auf dem Feld meines Vaters.
Ich sah den Tod in den Augen meines Freundes.
Ich streckte die Hand aus nach den Seelen der Ertrunkenen.
Ich bin müde . . .

Tired

I am tired . . .
With the trees I conversed.
With the sheep I suffered drought.
With the birds I sang in the woods.
I loved the girls in the village.
I looked up towards the sun.
I saw the sea.
I worked with the potter.
I breathed the dust on the country road.
I saw the blooms of melancholy on my father's field.
I saw death in the eyes of my friend.
I proffered my hand to the souls of the drowned.
I am tired . . .

Mit sechsundzwanzig Jahren

Sechsundzwanzig Jahre
der Wälder, des Ruhms und der Armut,
sechsundzwanzig Neujahrstage und keinen Freund
und den Tod
und immer wieder die Sonne
und kein Paar wasserdichte Schuhe gegen die Erschütterungen
                                        der Erde.
Sechsundzwanzig Jahre
wie im Traum, ein schlecht gesungener Choral
unter dem Wind im April,
und kein Haus und keine Mutter
und keine Vorstellung von Gott, dem Vater, der
                        aus den Taglöhnern spricht.
Sechsundzwanzig Jahre
unter Biersäufern, Heiligen, Mördern und Irren,
in der Stadt und in angeschwollenen Dörfern,
täglich erschaffen und täglich ausgespieen,
von Weihnacht zu Weihnacht schwankend,
kein Schuster, kein Gastwirt, kein Bettler,
ohne Gitarre und ohne Bibel,
im Oktober krank vor Heimweh,
im August todkrank vor Blumen.
Sechsundzwanzig Jahre,
die niemand erlebt hat,
kein Kind, kein Grab und keinen
Totengräber, mit dem ich reden könnte an einem Biertisch.
Sechsundzwanzig Jahre
in einer einzigen Ungerechtigkeit gegen alle,
versoffen unter den Mostfässern meines Vaters,
in faulen Tälern
verspielt und verlassen mit Gelächter,
nichts als Schnee und Finsternis
und die tiefen Spuren der Väter,
in denen meine tödliche Seele zurückstapft.

At Twenty-Six

Twenty-six years
of forests, glory and poverty,
twenty-six New Year's Days and no friend
and death
and time after time the sun
and no pair of watertight shoes against the convulsions of the earth.
Twenty-six years
as if in a dream, a badly sung chant
beneath the wind of April,
and no house and no mother
and no idea of God, the father, who speaks from the day laborers.
Twenty-six years
among beer drinkers, saints, murderers and madmen,
in the city and in the swollen villages,
created every day and spat out every day,
staggering from Christmas to Christmas,
no shoemaker, no innkeeper, no beggar,
without a guitar and without a bible,
in October homesick,
in August sick to death of flowers.
Twenty-six years
which no one has experienced,
no child, no grave and no
gravedigger that I could chat to at a beer table.
Twenty-six years
of one sole injustice against everyone,
drunk beneath my father's must vats,
in lazy valleys
frisky and forlorn with laughter,
nothing but snow and darkness
and the deep footprints of the fathers,
in which my deathly soul trudges back.

Wo des letzten Märzwinds Hauch
spürbar ist

Wir suchen die Toten
unter dem Gras und strecken die Finger
und haben keine Ruhe, morgen nicht und nicht übermorgen
und unter dem Baum und hinter den Hügeln
und über den einsamen Hohlwegen,
wo des letzten Märzwinds Hauch spürbar ist.

Früher klagten wir oft den Greis
und verachteten diese Kinder,
unsere Mutter verstand nicht und unser Vater,
und morgen und übermorgen, in tausend Jahren
werden wir fragen, wer da im Dunkeln
gestorben ist.

Wir suchen die Toten,
aus schwarzen Krügen trinken wir Fieber,
wir träumen den Mond und die Sterne
und trinken und tragen Trauer,
und führen Pferde und binden Säcke
und zimmern Särge und gehen schlafen.

Wir suchen die Toten
unter dem Gras und strecken die Finger
und finden nicht Ruhe, morgen nicht und übermorgen
und unter dem Baum und hinter den Hügeln
und über den einsamen Hohlwegen,
wo des letzten Märzwinds Hauch spürbar ist.

Where the Last Breath of March Wind
Is Felt

We seek the dead
beneath the grass, reach out our fingers
and have no rest, not tomorrow nor the day after,
beneath the tree or behind the hills
or through the forsaken ravines
where the last breath of March wind is felt.

We often used to accuse the old man
and scorn these children,
our mother didn't understand, nor our father,
and tomorrow, the day after, and in a thousand years' time
we shall ask who died here
in the dark.

We seek the dead
and drink fever from black tankards,
we dream the moon and the stars
and drink and wear mourning,
and lead horses and tie sacks
and knock up coffins and go to bed.

We seek the dead
beneath the grass, reach out our fingers
and find no rest, not tomorrow nor the day after,
beneath the tree or behind the hills
or through the forsaken ravines
where the last breath of March wind is felt.

Frühling der schwarzen Blüten

Frühling der schwarzen Blüten, dich treibt
der Toten Fieber,
Frühling der schwarzen Blüten, dich treibt
ein endloser Wind von Norden,
ein Grab ist mein April,
eine finstere Traumnacht der schwarzen Blüten,
dich treiben seltsame Schwestern ins Land,
wenn die Krähen schrein
und die Hügel Schauer trinken.

Frühling der schwarzen Blüten, dich treibt
der Toten Fieber,
Frühling der schwarzen Blüten, dich treibt
ein endloser Wind von Norden,
ich werde schlafen, morgen schon
wird mich Schnee und Einsamkeit zudecken hinter
                              deinen Schuhen . . .
dich treiben seltsame Schwestern ins Land,
wenn die Krähen schrein
und die Hügel Schauer trinken.

Spring of Black Blooms

Spring of black blooms, you're driven
by the fever of the dead,
spring of black blooms, you're driven
by an endless north wind,
my April is a grave,
a dark dream-night of black blooms,
you're driven by strange sisters, into the country,
when the crows cry
and the hills drink dread.

Spring of black blooms, you're driven
by the fever of the dead,
spring of black blooms, you're driven
by an endless north wind,
I shall sleep, and even tomorrow
snow and solitude will cover me, behind

                                    your shoes . . .
you're driven by strange sisters, into the country,
when the crows cry
and the hills drink dread.

Wehend sprach der Wind zu diesen Feldern

Wehend sprach der Wind zu diesen Feldern:
Tote kamen aus verlassnen Schenken,
türmten Fleisch vor schwarzen, tiefen Wäldern,
tranken ihrer letzten Tage Mühsal
in verbrannten, öden Sommertälern,

denn der Trauer folgen Totentage.
Die nicht liebten, waren bald vergessen,
doch sie sorgten sich um ihre Kränze
und verbrauchten abertausend irdne Krüge
in den Festen ihrer Müdigkeit.

Waren sie auch von der Nacht behütet,
ihrer Füße Spuren waren morgens
in den Lehm der Totenstadt gezeichnet;
draußen blühten spät die Apfelbäume,
Halme tanzten und der Wind aus Osten
sagte nichts von einer andern Welt.

Diese Tage kommen nicht mehr wieder,
nicht aus diesen Dörfern, diesen Städten.
Viele Inseln tragen ihre Namen.
Ihre Trauer aber sieht man abends
unterm Wolkenspiel nach Hause ziehn.

Blowing, the Wind Spoke to These Fields

Blowing, the wind spoke to these fields:
the dead emerged from deserted taverns,
piled up flesh on the edge of deep black forests,
and drank their last days' plight
in scorched and barren summer valleys,

for sorrow is followed by days of the dead.
Those who hadn't loved were soon forgotten,
yet they tended to their wreaths
and used up thousands upon thousands of crocks
in celebration of their weariness.

Though well-protected by the night,
the traces of their footprints were drawn
in the clay of the necropolis in the morning;
outside the apple trees blossomed late,
blades of grass danced and the easterly wind
said nothing of another world.

These days shall never come again,
not from these villages or these towns.
Many islands bear their names.
Yet their sorrow is seen in the evening,
on its way home beneath the play of clouds.

Herbst

Morgen kommt ihr wieder,
Bäcker, Schneider, Lügner,
Straßenkehrer,
der mir das Lied neidet,
das meine zerschlagene Seele singt.

Morgen kommt ihr wieder,
ihr Vögel, ihr Bäume, ihr wunderbaren
Kerker des Sommers,
den mein Vater geschickt hat
von den schwarzen Bergen.

Morgen kommt ihr wieder,
die meinen Ruhm in die Erde schreiben
unter den roten Kastanien,
und die mein Werk verachten und mein Blut,
das der Welt,
im Herbst.

Morgen kommt ihr wieder,
tote Freunde und welke Träume, –
eine Amsel hörst du, dein Schatten
läuft durch das Flußbett,
und nichts, kein Mensch
wird dich trösten.

Fall

Tomorrow you'll come again,
bakers, tailors, liars,
roadsweepers,
who envy me the song
that my shattered soul sings.

Tomorrow you'll come again,
you birds, you trees, you wonderful
dungeons of summer,
which my father sent
from the black mountains.

Tomorrow you'll come again,
you who write my glory in the earth
beneath the red chestnut trees,
and who scorn my work and my blood,
that of the world,
in the fall.

Tomorrow you'll come again,
dead friends and withered dreams—
you'll hear a blackbird, and your shadow
will run along the riverbed,
and nothing, no human being,
will console you.

Tod und Thymian

Nach Thymian und Tod roch die Erde,
    nach Heu und Wind,
aus dem Bach stieg die Seele der Mutter
    und ging über die Bäume wie zu Zeiten
des wolkenlosen, bitteren Frühjahrs.
    Nach Thymian und Tod roch die Erde
und niemand kam mit einem Korb,
    sie heimzutragen. –
Weil das Schwein zu kostbar ist,
    trugen sie keine Erde heim,
nicht die Erde, die nach Tod und Thymian roch.
    Ich schaute durch die Eichen
    hinunter ins Dorf.
Ich hörte die Kirchtagstrompeten
    und die Selchfleischposaunen,
und ich hörte die Würste krachen
    und die Bretter des Tanzbodens
im Gelächter des Priesters. –
    Auf einem Stein
schlief ich nach tausend Jahren.
    Niemand kam um ein Stück Erde,
das nach Tod und Thymian roch.

Death and Thyme

The earth smelled of thyme and death,
    of hay and wind,
my mother's soul rose from the stream
    and walked over the trees as in the days
of cloudless, bitter spring.
    The earth smelled of thyme and death,
and no one came with a basket
    to carry it home.—
Because the pig is too precious
    they carried home no earth,
no earth which smelled of death and thyme.
    Through the oak trees I watched
    the village below.
I heard country-fair trumpets
    and smoked-pork trombones,
and heard sausages crackle
    and the boards of the dance floor
in the laughter of the priest.—
    After a thousand years
I slept on a stone.
    No one came for a piece of earth
that smelled of death and thyme.

Brief an die Mutter

Du kommst in der Nacht, wenn die Magd ihre Brust aufmacht
   und der Apfelbaum leer ist
   und die Sterne meinen Namen zerstören,
Du kommst, wenn der Bach aufhört zu trauern und seine Worte
   einfrieren in meinem Fenster
   und die Schafe sich in die Stallecke flüchten vor meinem Gelächter,
Du kommst, wenn die Mitte der Welt
   einen Blutstrom ausspeit mit einem Seufzer,
Du kommst, wenn das Feld kahl ist und grün die Augen
   der Fische leuchten,
Du kommst, wenn keiner kommt, wenn sich die Magd,
                    die mir die Brüste gab,
   vor meinem Ruhm versteckt,
   wenn sie ihr Haar wie Jahrmillionen glitzern läßt im
                       Mondlicht,
Du kommst, wenn sie mich schlagen, ohne mein Gebet zu kennen,
   das ich sprechen werde mit den Anfangsworten: »Ich bin
   von der Finsternis getrieben . . .«
Du kommst immer, wenn ich müde bin. Ich zahle dir
   mein Leben zurück mit der Angst,
   die auf deinem widersinnigen Grabstein zerfällt
   über der großen Lüge des Herbstes.

Letter to my Mother

You come in the night, when the girl bares her breast
    and the apple tree is empty
    and the stars destroy my name,
you come when the stream ceases to mourn and its words
    freeze in my window
    and the sheep flee from my laughter into a corner of the barn,
you come when the middle of the world
    spews out a stream of blood with a sigh,
you come when the field is bare and the eyes of the fish
    glow green,
you come when no one comes, when the girl
                     who gave me her breasts,
    hides from my glory,
    when she lets her hair sparkle in the moonlight,
                     like millions of years
you come when they beat me, without knowing the prayer
    that I shall speak, beginning with the words: "I was driven
    by the darkness . . ."
You always come when I'm tired. I repay you
    for my life with the fear
    that molders on your absurd gravestone
    above the great lie of autumn.

Die heute tot sind

Die heute tot sind, kommen zu Gelagen, daß
dir der Gaumen schäumt und dir die Erde
niederträchtig erscheint, die dich nicht Wein
und Sommer und süßes Fleisch erfühlen läßt,
die wunderbaren Keller der Verfaulten,
die ihre Gräber ungebrochen überschatten,
als heulten nicht am Wald die Wächterhunde.

Aus faulen Unterständen herauf, wie aus den Höllen
der Väter, vergraben, vergraben und von Trauer
träg, schrein in der Nacht die abgestorbenen Glieder
der Menschen, doch waren ihre Leiber
am Glück des Sterbens längst verfault und
ohne Glanz, weil sie von ihren Händlern
bedeckt waren und kaum von Meer und Niedertrachten satt.

Wie fielen da die Steine auf ihre Arme, die
nach Jubel lebten und nach Heiterkeit und vollen
Krügen der Totenmähler—Musik der strahlenden Skelette,
und Hunger nach Vergängnis trieb sie wie ein Heer
zerfallner Sommer durch die finstern Gänge,
und aus den Tälern hörten wir die Laute
der stummen Krieger, die gefallen waren
für einen Stein, für einen Schwanz und eine Hure.

Die Gänge sind so tief, daß du sie nicht durchschreiten
und nicht zerstören kannst mit dem Gelächter
der Fürsten und Gebärenden der Erde,
und ihre Schenkel tönen wie Musik in Elendsställen,
die deiner Qual den dumpfen Zorn der Tiere
entgegen tragen. Verrat, Verrat, o bittere Vergängnis
des Frühlings hinter grauen, abgeschlagenen Hufen,
wo kein Gewächs der Finsternis dich treibt über die Berge.

Those Who Are Dead Today

Those who are dead today arrive at feasts
that would make your palate foam, and make
the earth, which does not let you feel the wine
and summer and sweet flesh, seem mean,
the wonderful cellars of the decomposed
casting undaunted a pall over their graves,
as if watchdogs were not howling at the woods.

From rotten bunkers, as if risen from the hells
of our fathers, buried, buried and weary with
sorrow, dead human limbs scream in the night,
though their bodies, long since decayed
from the bliss of dying, have no sheen
because covered over by their tradesmen
and barely sated by sea and meanness.

How the stones here fell on their arms,
which lived for rejoicing, merriness and the full
tankards of funeral banqueters—the music of radiant skeletons
and hunger for transience drove them like an army
of crumbled summers through dark passages,
and from the valleys we heard the sounds
of the silent warriors who had fallen
for a stone, for a cock and a whore.

Passages so deep that you cannot pass through them
nor destroy them with the laughter
of the princes and child-bearers of this earth,
and their thighs sound like music in squalid stables,
bearing the muffled rage of the animals
for your torment. Betrayal, betrayal, O bitter transience
of spring behind gray chipped hoofs, where no growth
of darkness drives you over the mountains.

Ich habe sie gesehn im Winter, und seh sie heute noch
an ihren Füßen Melancholie und schwarzen Kummer tragen,
hinunter in die Städte, die aufgerissnen Plätze, die ein Sommerwind
in seiner Reinheit überf.hrt, in kranke Täler, die das nasse Gras
zum Himmel strecken, in die Welt, in Häfen, Finsternisse,
                         Äcker, deren Samen
nach den erbrochnen Himmeln stinkt der Menschen; Augenblicke
wie Moos, das unterm Mond zurücktritt in Vergessenheit, in
irgendeines Maurers oder Töpfers Tagewerk.

Von Inseln sprach da keiner in der Nacht und keiner zahlte,
wenn dir die Wirte ihren Speck aufdrängten, die Poesien
der Gasterei, über dem Fluß gehäuft und von viel
                         Honig und viel
Hunger nach der geträumten Erde duftend, in einer Welt, die
deiner eignen nur in den Gedärmen glich; sie sprachen nicht
von Hunderten von Häusern, Gräbern, Hügeln, Brücken, die
deine Trauer waren, nicht von Schönheit—doch sie prahlten alle,
und ihre Schläfen sanken ununterbrochen und ohne Frieden
hinunter in Vergessenheit, in Kot und Wasser, schwarz,
                         das keiner liebte.

I saw them in winter and still see them today,
bearing at their feet melancholy and black anxiety
down to the towns, whose lacerated squares a summer wind
in all its purity, traverses, to the sick valleys, stretching wet grass
to the sky, the world, in prisons, eclipses, and fields
whose seeds
stink to vomited heaven of human beings; moments
like moss beneath the moon, receding into oblivion,
to some mason's or potter's daily work.

No one there in the night spoke of islands, and no one paid
when the publicans foisted their bacon upon you, the poetry
of innkeeping, heaped above the river, smelling sweetly
of so much honey and
so much hunger for the imagined earth; they said nothing
of the hundreds of houses, graves, hills and bridges which made up
your sorrow, nor of beauty—yet they all boasted,
and their temples sank constantly, without peace,
down into oblivion, into excrement and water, black,
that no one loved.

RÜCKKEHR IN EINE LIEBE

✳

RETURN TO A LOVE

Yeats war nicht dabei

(Der irische Dichter William Butler
Yeats rühmt in seinen Versen oft die
Rückkehr in die ländliche Heimat)

Meinen Namen
    nehmen die Äcker nicht an,
die Wiesen schicken mein Leben
    zurück in die Städte;
die Bäume ziehn ihre Wurzeln zurück,
    die Bäche schließen den Mund,
wenn ich ins Dorf
    zum Grab der Mutter geh'.
Keiner gibt mir den Krug und sagt,
    ich soll ihn austrinken,
keiner macht sein Bett auf
    für mich.
Wenn sie wüßten, wie
    mich friert!
In den Wäldern und
    hinter dem Haus
bezichtigen sie mich der Lüge.

Yeats Wasn't There

(In his poetry, the Irish poet
William Butler Yeats often extols
returning to his rural homeland)

The fields
    do not assume my name,
the meadows send my life
    back to the towns;
the trees retract their roots,
    the streams close their mouths,
when I visit the village
    and my mother's grave.
No one hands me a tankard and
    tells me to drink up,
no one offers me
    a bed for the night.
If only they knew
    how cold I feel!
In the woods and
    behind the house
they accuse me of lying.

Rückkehr in eine Liebe

Die Berge rückten her und sprachen nur vom Sterben
und viele Tote gaben einer Amsel das Geleit und blieben stumm
bis weit hinunter in die ausweglosen Städte . . .
. . . nur das Mühlrad klagte, klagte so, als wären diese Wasser
einsamer noch, als du sie wieder sahst in dieser Kammer,
wo sich
der Duft des Korns mit ihren Phantasien mischte.

Wie kam ich her? Beinahe sah ich nicht, wie mich mein
eignes Fleisch auffraß.
Sie rief mich oft . . . War's aus dem Süden? War's
aus dem kalten Land? War's eine Stimme, die
mein Vaterland mißachtete?
Ich weiß kein Glück, das ferner ist als diese Liebe.

Vögel schwärzten mir die Winterzüge meiner Einsamkeit
und brachten Botschaft von verlassenen Bordellen, Wein
und Kinderleichen, die der Traurigkeit – durch meine
Nächte gingen ihre Schritte.
Der Schnee verfolgte mich mit seiner vernichtenden Poesie.

Return to a Love

As the mountains moved in, they spoke only of dying,
while many of the dead escorted a blackbird away, all staying silent
till far below in the dead-end towns . . .
. . . only the millwheel lamented, lamenting as if these waters
were still more lonely than when you saw them again,
                                        in this room where the
smell of corn mingled with their daydreams.

How did I get here? I almost missed seeing how my own
                                        flesh devoured me.
She called me often . . . Was it from the south? Was it
from the cold country? Was it a voice which
flouted my fatherland?
I know no joy that is further removed than this love.

Birds blackened the winter migrations of my loneliness
and brought news of deserted brothels, wine
and children's corpses, their sadness—and their steps
                                        passed through my nights.
The snow pursued me with its crushing poetry.

Vor dem Apfelbaum

Ich sterbe nicht, bevor ich die Kuh gesehen habe
    im Stall meines Vaters,
bevor das Gras nicht meine Zunge säuert
    und die Milch mein Leben verändert.
Ich sterbe nicht, bevor der Rand meines Kruges voll ist
    und die Liebe meiner Schwester mich erinnert,
wie schön unser Tal ist,
    In dem sie die Butter kneten
und Zeichen in den Speck schneiden zu Ostern . . .
    Ich sterbe nicht, bevor der Wald seine Stürme schickt
und die Bäume vom Sommer reden,
    bevor die Mutter auf der Straße geht mit einem roten Tuch,
hinter dem holprigen Karren, auf dem sie
    ihr Glück schiebt: Äpfel, Birnen, Hühner und Stroh –
Ich sterbe nicht, bevor die Tür zufällt, durch
    die ich gekommen bin
vor dem Apfelbaum –

On the Apple Tree

I shall not die before I see the cow
    in my father's cowshed,
not before the grass sours my tongue
    and the milk changes my life.
I shall not die before my tankard is full to the brim
    and my sister's love reminds me
how beautiful our valley is,
    where they knead the butter
and carve signs in the bacon for Easter . . .
    I shall not die before the forest sends its storms
and the trees talk of summer,
    before mother goes out on the road with a red cloth
behind the clumsy cart she pushes
    with her luck: apples, pears, chickens and straw—
I shall not die before the door through
    which I came closes
on the apple tree—

In das Dorf muß ich zurück

In das Dorf muß ich zurück, in dem ich aufwuchs,
    an den Fluß, der meine Gräber bespült,
an die Seele des Hauses, in dem mein Vater den Wein
    züchtete und das Leben seiner Kinder,
wo im Tuffstein eingemeißelt steht: »Hau dich hin zu
                    Most und Totenschinken.«
    In das Dorf muß ich zurück, in dem sie mich
                beschmutzten mit ihren Sprüchen,
in die Nacht, die nach dem Heu des Hungers schmeckt,
    in den Schatten, der den Hügel auffrißt,
in die Finsternis der Gedankenblöcke, auf denen mein
           Name steht, der Name des Sterblichen.
    In das Dorf muß ich zurück, das mein Heimweh mißbrauchte,
in dem sie Milch zu Wasser schlugen,
    in dem sie die Sterne zerstörten mit ihrem Gelächter.
In das Dorf muß ich zurück, in dem
    die Schuhe meines Vaters ausgelöscht sind,
in dem meine Mutter verhungert ist im letzten Kriegsjahr,
    in dem die Fische leuchten wie der einzige Himmel!
In das Dorf muß ich zurück, wo der Hafer steht wie die Sonne,
    wo die Kühe gehen,
wo die Bäche verkünden, wie herrlich die Angst vor den Städten ist,
    wo der Krug sich füllt mit Tau und Eifersucht.
In dieses Dorf muß ich zurück,
    bevor ich tot bin,
und vom Wind zerfressen, der mein Zeichen trägt.

To the Village I Must Return

I must return to the village where I was born,
    to the river that laps my graves,
to the soul of the house where my father cultivated
    his wine and his children's lives,
and in the tufa is inscribed: "Get down to the cider
                    and the ham of the dead."
    I must return to the village where they soiled me
                   with their sayings,
to the night that tastes of the hay of hunger,
    to the shadow that devours the hill,
to the gloom of the blocks of thought on which
        my name is written, the name of a mortal.
    I must return to the village that abused my homesickness
by beating the milk to water,
    by destroying the stars with its laughter.
I must return to the village in which
    my father's shoes were destroyed,
where my mother starved to death in the last year of the war,
    where the fish gleam like the one and only heaven!
I must return to the village where the oats stand like the sun,
    where the cows walk,
where the streams proclaim how glorious it is to fear the towns,
    where the tankard fills with dew and jealousy.
To this village I must return
    before I am dead
and devoured by the wind that bears my sign.

Der Wind

Der Wind kommt in der Nacht
    und trägt mich zurück in die Dörfer,
in das dumpfe Geräusch der Buttertröge.

Der Wind kommt in der Nacht,
    er wickelt meinen Namen in die Kastanienblätter
und treibt ihn nach Norden.

Der Wind kommt in der Nacht
    vor dem Gesicht der Sonne,
die meinen Bruder entführt hat.

Der Wind kommt in der Nacht,
    sein Schmerzensschrei wirbelt
in unzähligen Kronen,

der Schrei, den mein Vater noch nicht gekannt hat,
    der Wind, der Wind, der Wind,

    der die Toten einsammelt,
der die Haustüren aufreißt,
    der meine Seele treibt,

der Wind, der Wind, der Wind.

The Wind

The wind comes in the night
    and carries me back to the villages,
to the hollow sound of the butter vats.

The wind comes in the night,
    it wraps my name in chestnut leaves
and propels it northwards.

The wind comes in the night
    before the face of the sun
which abducted my brother.

The wind comes in the night
    its cry of pain swirling
in countless crowns,

the cry that my father had not yet known,
    the wind, the wind, the wind

    which gathers the dead together,
which rips open the front doors,
    which propels my soul,

the wind, the wind, the wind.

Nachts kehrt der Duft der Büsche zurück

Nachts kehrt der Duft der Büsche zurück.
Die Seelen huschen aus schwarzen Zimmern.
Wir aber schlafen und träumen und wissen nicht,
war das der Vater? War das die Mutter?
War das der Frühling, der ging vorbei?

Nachts hängen Sterne wie Tropfen Bluts.
Das Wasser des Flusses gräbt sich ins Grab.
Wir aber schlafen und träumen und wissen nicht,
war das der Vater? War das die Mutter?

Nachts steht ein Toter am Feldrain auf.
Er schreitet zum Wein und zum bitteren Brot.
Wir aber schlafen und träumen und wissen nicht,
war das der Vater? War das die Mutter?
War das der Frühling, der ging vorbei?

Nachts gehen Fischer mit nassen Netzen
hinter das Meer in ein trauriges Land.
Wir aber schlafen und träumen und wissen nicht,
war das der Vater? War das die Mutter?

At Night the Scent of the Bushes Returns

At night the scent of the bushes returns.
Souls flit out of black rooms.
Yet we sleep and dream, knowing nothing.
Was that our father? Was it our mother?
Was it spring that passed by?

At night the stars hang like drops of blood.
The water of the river digs down to its grave.
Yet we sleep and dream, knowing nothing.
Was that our father? Was it our mother?

At night, rising from the edge of the field,
a dead man heads for wine and bitter bread.
Yet we sleep and dream, knowing nothing.
Was that our father? Was it our mother?
Was it spring that passed by?

At night the fishermen walk with wet nets
beyond the sea to a land of sadness.
Yet we sleep and dream, knowing nothing.
Was that our father? Was it our mother?

Vor dem Dorf

Die Gesichter, die aus dem Feld tauchen, fragen
    mich nach der Rückkunft.
Mein Schrei stört nicht die Schwalbe,
    die auf dem zerbrochenen Ast hockt. Finster
ist meine Seele, die der Wind treibt
    ans Meer, zu riechen das Salz der Erde.
Meine Legende ist sterblich.
    Unter dem Baum, der meinem Bruder ähnlich ist,
zähl ich die Sterne der Schiffer.

Outside the Village

The faces that emerge from the field ask
    me about my return.
My scream does not disturb the swallow
    perching on the broken bough. Gloomy
is my soul, which the wind propels
    to the sea, to smell the salt of the earth.
My legend is mortal.
    Beneath the tree that resembles my brother,
I count the mariners' stars.

Am Brunnen

Der Mond schaut aus dem Brunnen.
    Wer wird
seine Augen heimtragen für den Winter,
    wenn der Schnee die Erde zudeckt?
    Wer wird
meinen Namen sprechen, die Blüten wiedersehn,
    die der Regen treibt?
    Wer wird
mich trösten, wenn die Seelen der Bäume
    versteint sind in tausend Jahren?
    Wer wird
meiner Verlassenheit einen Grabstein setzen
    und nicht nach meiner Welt fragen?
    Wer wird
die Vögel lieben, die ich verachte,
    weil sie nach Süden ziehn?

At the Well

The moon peers out from the well.
    Who will
carry its eyes home for winter
    when snow covers the earth?
    Who will
utter my name and see again the blossoms
    borne by the rain?
    Who will
comfort me when the souls of the trees
    are petrified in a thousand years time?
    Who will
set up a gravestone to my desolation
    and not enquire about my world?
    Who will
love the birds that I despise
    because they migrate south?

Der Tod

Der Tod hat mich ins Sommerheu geschlagen.
    Jetzt hängt er draußen und lacht
und erwürgt den Birnbaum.
    Niemand schüttelt ihn herunter,
kein Trompetenstoß
    verscheucht ihn zu den Hügeln,
aus den Tälern kommen sie, die mich erschlagen werden;
    Bauern, Händler, Fleischer
und der Pfarrer mit dem Osterlamm,
    der sich mir anvertraut.
Der Tod hat mich ins Sommerheu geschlagen.
    Keiner bricht mir
meinen Ruhm entzwei und läßt mich laufen . . .

Death

Death has beaten me into the summer hay.
   Now he hangs outside laughing
and strangling the pear tree.
   No one shakes him down,
no trumpet blast
   chases him off to the hills,
from the valleys they'll come, those who will slay me;
   farmers, tradesmen, butchers
and the priest with his Easter lamb,
   who confides in me.
Death has beaten me into the summer hay.
   No one breaks my
glory in twain and lets me go free . . .

Altentann

Der Tag zieht sein Hemd aus.
    Nackt steigt er ins Gartenbeet
und ruft die Vögel zusammen.
    In den schwarzen Pfützen
hockt sein rotes Gesicht,
    das die Bauern zerschlagen haben.
Das Gras sticht Schattenlanzen
    in mein Hirn –

Auf dem Nachbarfenster
    sitzt ein Vogel
wie der Hüter meiner Gedanken,
    bis der derbe Schlaf
mir die nassen Schuhe auszieht.

Altentann

Day takes its shirt off.
    Naked it climbs into the flowerbed
and summons the birds.
    In the black puddles
it crouches, red face
    battered by farmers.
The grass jabs shadow lances
    into my brain—

At my neighbor's window
    sits a bird
like the keeper of my thoughts,
    till rude sleep
takes my wet shoes off.

Im Weizen ist mein Herz

Im Weizen ist mein Herz, rot
   wie das Land,
schön und verrückt wie die Erde,
   die mich tötet.

Ich sehe im Osten den Vater
   jung, mit rotem Tuch
und nackten Füßen,
   die über mein Heimweh gehn.

Ich sehe die Mutter stehn an meinem Grab
   alt und zerbrechlich,
das Blut tropft
   von ihrer Wange
in meine Vergänglichkeit.

In the Wheat Is My Heart

In the wheat is my heart, red
    like the land,
beautiful and crazy like the earth
    which kills me.

In the east I see my father,
    young, with a red scarf,
and naked feet
    that walk upon my homesickness.

I see my mother standing at my grave,
    old and brittle,
blood dripping
    from her cheek
into my transience.

Elternhaus

Sie sind nicht mehr da,
    mich führen andere Redensarten hinunter
zum Fleisch und zum Wein,
    mich treiben andere Sprüche
in ihre verlassenen Zimmer,
    es geht der Wind nur bis zum zerschundenen Haustor,
der Speck und das Schweigen
    sind übrig geblieben,
und alle Verse, die sie in langer Nacht sprachen,
    verwesen im andern Land
hinter diesen Bergen,
    wo der Frühe seltsamer Zauber
die Bauern zum Suff treibt.
    Sie sind nicht mehr da,
mich friert wie den Hund vom Bäcker,
    der seinen Schwanz an der Mauer reibt,
mich friert und schlafen
    kann ich nicht mehr.
Meine Lieder sind ausgetrocknet
    so wie das Flußbett im grauen Sommer,
der seine Klagen
    hinunter schiebt an das Meer.
Sie sind nicht mehr da,
    ich möchte schlafen
und träumen von ihnen, die mir
    ein Fleisch und Erinnerung gaben,
    die schwarzen Lebzeiten,
den Hunger trauriger Hirne,
    und müden Duft der Wälder
und faulen Ruhm der Welt.
Ich will jetzt schlafen
    und ihr Grabmal sehn.

My Parents' Home

They are no longer here,
    other figures of speech lead me down
to the flesh and the wine,
    other sayings drive me
into their deserted rooms,
    the wind blows as far as the chafed front door,
the bacon and the silence
    have remained,
and all the verses they recited in the long night
    decay in the other land
beyond the mountains,
    where early morning's strange magic
drives farmers to drink.
    They are no longer there,
I'm as cold as the baker's dog
    which rubs its tail against the wall,
I'm cold
    and can no longer sleep.
My songs have dried up
    like the river bed in gray summer,
which sends its lament
    down to the sea.
They are no longer here,
    I'd like to sleep
and dream of them, they who gave me
    flesh and memory,
    black lifetimes,
the hunger of sad brains,
    the tired scent of the woods
and the lazy glory of the world.
I shall sleep now
    and view their tomb.

Mein Vater

Mein Vater litt an der Dürre der Erde
wie an dem zerfallnen Gesicht des Sommers,
er stieg den Berg hinauf und rastete über den Tümpeln.
Damals fuhren die Schiffe gegen Westen,
niemals werde ich vergessen, wie des Vaters Hand
nach der menschlichen Seele griff –
Er stieg den Berg hinauf, um das Land zu sehen, das sie
zertrampelt haben in sieben Wochen.
»Ich sage euch«, sagte er, »unzerstörbar ist die Liebe –.«
Dann rollten die Panzer über das Weizenfeld und begruben
die Hoffnung auf das kommende Jahr.
Sie litten alle an der Dürre der Erde, manche
fielen zurück in die Nacht, sie sagten: wir
finden keine Strophe in diesem ungeheuren Vers.
Mein Vater glaubte, diese Erde gehöre ihm, denn er hatte
sich hundert Joch gekauft und eine Hütte mit
Bäumen; darin schlief er,
aber er fand keinen Traum.
Hundert Millionen Jahre sah er in den Augen der Tiere,
die in der Weihnacht flackerten.
Er sagte: »Wir brauchen keine Kerzen!«
Mein Vater brach den Zweig vom Ölbaum und trug Schnee
an die Lippen seiner Schwestern.
In Sibirien schiffte er sich ein für die Reise, doch
brauchte er eine Ewigkeit, denn sie litten alle
an der Dürre der Erde,
und eine Stimme sagte in ihm: »Ich werde mein Licht
in den menschlichen Schnee tauchen.«

My Father

My father suffered from the aridity of the earth,
likewise from the moldered face of summer,
he climbed the mountain and rested above the tarns.
At that time the ships used to sail westwards,
never shall I forget how my father's hand
reached out for the human soul—
He climbed the mountain to see the countryside that they
trampled to bits in seven weeks.
"I tell you", he said, "Love is indestructible—."
Then the tanks rolled over the wheat field and buried
hope for the coming year.
They all suffered from the aridity of the earth, some
fell back into the night, saying: we
cannot find any verses at all in this monstrous poem.
My father believed this earth belonged to him, since he
had bought a hundred acres and a hut with
trees; in which he slept,
but found no dream.
For hundreds of millions of years he gazed into the animals' eyes
as they flickered on Christmas Eve.
He said: "We don't need candles!"
My father brought a branch from the olive tree and carried snow
to the lips of his sisters.
In Siberia he embarked upon a voyage, yet
needed an eternity, because they were all suffering
from the aridity of the earth,
and a voice within him said: "I shall dip my light
in the human snow."

In den Friedhof gehn meine Füße

In den Friedhof gehn meine Füße,
tausend Jahre in den Friedhof hinein,
in die Erde, die nach dem Mörtel der Geister riecht,
nach den Fingern der Zigeuner.
In den Friedhof gehn meine Füße,
tausend Jahre in den Friedhof hinein,
in den Wind,
in die Stimmen der Erde.
In den Friedhof gehn meine Füße,
tausend Jahre in den Friedhof hinein,
in den Brunnen des Lärms,
in das Fleisch,
in die Steine, die auf den Herzen liegen und sie erdrücken,
in die schwarzen Krüge,
aus denen der Wein
der Selcher und Totengräber,
der Wein der Bauerngötter heraufsteigt.

My Feet Walk into the Graveyard

My feet walk into the graveyard,
a thousand years into the graveyard,
into the earth that smells of the mortar of spirits,
of the fingers of gypsies.
My feet walk into the graveyard,
a thousand years into the graveyard,
into the wind,
into the voices of the earth.
My feet walk into the graveyard,
a thousand years into the graveyard,
into the well of noise,
into the flesh,
into the stones that lie on hearts and crush them,
into the black tankards
from which the wine
of the butchers and gravediggers,
the wine of country gods, ascends.

Im Garten der Mutter

Im Garten der Mutter
sammelt mein Rechen die Sterne,
die herabgefallen sind, während ich fort war.
Die Nacht ist warm und meine Glieder
strömen die grüne Herkunft aus,
Blumen und Blätter,
den Amselruf und das Klatschen des Webstuhls.
Im Garten der Mutter
trete ich barfuß auf die Schlangenköpfe,
die durch das rostige Tor hereinschaun
mit feurigen Zungen.

In My Mother's Garden

In my mother's garden
my rake scrapes together the stars
that have fallen while I was away.
The night is warm and my limbs
emanate my green ancestry,
flowers and leaves,
the call of the blackbird and the clack of the loom.
In my mother's garden
I step barefoot on the serpents' heads
which drop in through the rusty gate
with fiery tongues.

Künftig werde ich in den Wald gehen

Künftig werde ich in den Wald gehen
und die Städte vergraben und die Nacht bändigen
mit dem Messer der Schwermut.
Ich werde durch die Wiesen gehen am Fronleichnamstag
und meine Wange ins Gras drücken
und meine Finger in den Rachen der Erde stecken.
Meine Nacht aber wird so sein: ohne Feuer und ohne Salz
werde ich auf den Steinen
meiner verlassenen Ortschaft knien
und meinen Vater suchen –
Ich werde an den Eutern der Kühe horchen und die
                              Kübel raunen hören,
    die vollgemolkenen.

In Future I Shall Walk in the Forest

In future I shall walk in the forest
and bury the towns and tame the night
with the knife of melancholy.
I shall walk through the meadows on Corpus Christi
and press my cheek to the grass
and stick my finger down the earth's throat.
Yet my night shall be like this: without fire and without salt
I shall kneel on the stones
of my deserted village
and seek my father –
I shall put my ear to the udders of the cows and hear
                                        the buckets murmur,

    full after milking.

Ich weiß, daß in den Büschen die Seelen sind

Ich weiß, daß in den Büschen die Seelen sind
von meinen Vätern,
im Korn
ist der Schmerz meines Vaters
und im großen schwarzen Wald.
Ich weiß, daß ihre Leben, die ausgelöscht sind
vor unseren Augen,
in den Ähren eine Zuflucht haben,
in der blauen Stirn des Junihimmels.
Ich weiß, daß die Toten
die Bäume sind und die Winde,
das Moos und die Nacht,
die ihre Schatten
auf meinen Grabhügel legt.

In the Bushes, I Know, Are the Souls

In the bushes, I know, are the souls
of my fathers,
in the corn
is the pain of my father
and in the great black forest.
I know that their lives, erased
before our very eyes,
have found refuge in the ears of corn,
in the blue brow of the June sky.
I know that the dead
are the trees and the winds,
the moss, and the night
which lays its shadows
upon my burial mound.

Notes: Some Remarks on the English Translation of
Auf der Erde und in der Hölle

In keeping with his interest in the tradition and poetic practices of Symbolism, Expressionism, and in particular the work of Georg Trakl (see above), Thomas Bernhard adopts in *Auf der Erde und in der Hölle* the stylistic mannerism of repeating certain key words, phrases, and images, either in one and the same poem or in several of them. I have tried, as far as possible to recreate this effect by retaining the recurrent equivalents in English. However, it has not always been possible to maintain this principle, due to the surrounding context diverging too far from the relevance of the repeated word, phrase, or image. I have therefore sometimes been forced to adopt alternative solutions at certain places throughout the book of poems.

Typically recurrent usages with Traklian connotations include the adjective *verlassen*, usually meaning "desolate" or "abandoned," "forlorn" or "forsaken," with the intimation of "lonely" and "solitary" often there in the background, and the abstract noun *Verlassenheit* meaning "desolation" or "abandonment." Further, *Verzweifelter* and *verzweifelt* mean (someone who is) "desperate," "in despair," "despairing," "frantic," "distraught," or "confused," while the noun *Verzweiflung* means "desperation." Still more Traklian is the use of *zerfallen*, basically meaning "decayed," but further "decomposed," "fallen into ruin," "crumbled" or "moldered."

The German word *Ruhm* not only means "glory," as I have almost always translated it here, but also "fame," which although it does not fit the context of the poems in their English translations, is sometimes carried along as a secondary association in German. In the original we therefore also gain this impression of the ambitious young poet eager to achieve glory and/or fame. It can also mean "splendor."

The German word *Stadt* could be translated by either "town" or "city." Unless the reference is definitely to a real city, such as Paris, I have usually adopted the former ("town") as being slightly more useful in indicating the nature of the difference between the rural life of a farming community centered upon a village and life in a town of whatever size. However, there may still be instances where a case may be made for use of the word "city."

In German, the word *Truhe* means "chest," yet here it is used in a rather strange way. By association it might indicate a "trunk" or "traveling chest," a "treasure chest," or a chest in which clothes, mementos, junk, or almost anything else are kept. However, in the poem "On the Black Chests of Country Earth" the connection is with a "chest of earth," moreover a chest of "country earth." Further associations extend to "box," "coffer," and even "coffin," yet the meaning of "chest" remains the primary one, despite (or perhaps because of) the surrealistic nature of the image.

Bauer or related words including the adjectival noun prefix *Bauern* generally mean "farmer" or "farming" today, yet in combinations can also be translated as "country," which is mostly the translation that has been adopted here. However, the word nexus also includes the derogatory historical connotation of "peasant."

© Peter Waugh
Vienna, Austria
2015

RECENT AND FORTHCOMING BOOKS FROM THREE ROOMS PRESS

FICTION

Meagan Brothers
Weird Girl and What's His Name

Ron Dakron
Hello Devilfish!

Michael T. Fournier
Hidden Wheel
Swing State

Janet Hamill
Tales from the Eternal Café
(Introduction by Patti Smith)

Eamon Loingsigh
Light of the Diddicoy
Exile on Bridge Street

Aram Saroyan
Still Night in L.A.

Richard Vetere
The Writers Afterlife
Champagne and Cocaine

MEMOIR & BIOGRAPHY

Nassrine Azimi and
Michel Wasserman
Last Boat to Yokohama:
The Life and Legacy of
Beate Sirota Gordon

James Carr
BAD: The Autobiography of
James Carr

Richard Katrovas
Raising Girls in Bohemia:
Meditations of an American Father;
A Memoir in Essays

Judith Malina
Full Moon Stages: Personal Notes
from 50 Years of The Living Theatre

Stephen Spotte
My Watery Self:
Memoirs of a Marine Scientist

HUMOR

Peter Carlaftes
A Year on Facebook

PHOTOGRAPHY-MEMOIR

Mike Watt
On & Off Bass

SHORT STORY ANTHOLOGY

Dark City Lights: New York Stories
edited by Lawrence Block

Have a NYC I, II & III:
New York Short Stories;
edited by Peter Carlaftes
& Kat Georges

Quarter-Life Crisis:
An Anthology of Millenial Writers
edited by Constance Renfrow

This Way to End Times:
Classic and New Stories of
the Apocalypse
edited by Robert Silverberg

MIXED MEDIA

John S. Paul
Sign Language: A Painter's
Notebook (photography, poetry
and prose)

TRANSLATIONS

Thomas Bernhard
On Earth and in Hell
(poems of Thomas Bernhard
with English translations by
Peter Waugh)

Patrizia Gattaceca
Isula d'Anima / Soul Island
(poems by the author
in Corsican with English
translations)

César Vallejo | Gerard Malanga
Malanga Chasing Vallejo
(selected poems of César Vallejo
with English translations
and additional notes by
Gerard Malanga)

George Wallace
EOS: Abductor of Men
(selected poems of George
Wallace with Greek translations)

DADA

Maintenant: A Journal of
Contemporary Dada Writing & Art
(Annual, since 2008)

FILM & PLAYS

Israel Horovitz
My Old Lady: Complete Stage Play
and Screenplay with an Essay on
Adaptation

Peter Carlaftes
Triumph For Rent (3 Plays)
Teatrophy (3 More Plays)

POETRY COLLECTIONS

Hala Alyan
Atrium

Peter Carlaftes
DrunkYard Dog
I Fold with the Hand I Was Dealt

Thomas Fucaloro
It Starts from the Belly and Blooms
Inheriting Craziness is Like
a Soft Halo of Light

Kat Georges
Our Lady of the Hunger

Robert Gibbons
Close to the Tree

Israel Horovitz
Heaven and Other Poems

David Lawton
Sharp Blue Stream

Jane LeCroy
Signature Play

Philip Meersman
This is Belgian Chocolate

Jane Ormerod
Recreational Vehicles on Fire
Welcome to the Museum of Cattle

Lisa Panepinto
On This Borrowed Bike

George Wallace
Poppin' Johnny

Three Rooms Press | New York, NY | Current Catalog: www.threeroomspress.com
Three Rooms Press books are distributed by PGW/Perseus: www.pgw.com